D0097761

A Mother's Garden of Prayer, tenderly written by godly women of prayer, will encourage mothers and grandmothers to pray and remind them of the power of prayer in family life. This little gem will mentor you in praying for your children in life situations, using Scripture-guided prayers.

—ESTHER BURROUGHS, SPEAKER AND AUTHOR

Sarah Maddox and Patti Webb have made an enormous contribution in *A Mother's Garden of Prayer* as they show us how to pray Scripture over our children at crucial moments and during critical events in their lives. Your own life will be changed and your children will be greatly blessed, protected, and guided.

—CAROL ANN AND JIMMY DRAPER;
DR. DRAPER IS PRESIDENT OF LIFEWAY CHRISTIAN RESOURCES

A Mother's Garden of Prayer is saturated with Scripture and all the suggested prayers are based on Scripture. I found myself constantly praying for my grandchildren as I read this book. Every mother should have this book handy while rearing children. I will continue to profit from it for a long time—and I am a father and grandfather.

—T.W. HUNT, AUTHOR OF *THE MIND OF CHRIST*

Sarah Maddox and Patti Webb have provided a valuable guidebook of intercession for mothers in the lives of their children. Not only will this book touch the hearts of moms everywhere, it will also serve as a prayer guide for every situation facing your child. We heartily recommend *A Mother's Garden of Prayer*.

—JO BETH AND ED YOUNG;
DR. YOUNG IS PASTOR OF SECOND BAPTIST CHURCH IN HOUSTON, TEXAS

A MOTHER'S GARDEN *of* PRAYER
CULTIVATING A LIFESTYLE OF PRAYING FOR YOUR CHILDREN

SARAH MADDOX *&* PATTI WEBB

BROADMAN
&HOLMAN
PUBLISHERS

Nashville, Tennessee

0-8054-1768-0

Published by Broadman & Holman Publishers, Nashville, Tennessee
Editorial Team: Vicki Crumpton, Janis Whipple, Kim Overcash
Page Design: Paul T. Gant Art & Design
Illustrations: Jim Hsieh
Typesetting: Desktop Miracles

Dewey Decimal Classification: 242
Subject Heading: MOTHERS—PRAYER-BOOKS AND DEVOTIONS / GRANDMOTHERS—
PRAYER-BOOKS AND DEVOTIONS / CHILDREN—RELIGIOUS LIFE
Library of Congress Card Catalog Number: 98-31067

Unless otherwise stated all Scripture citation is from the NASB, the New American Standard Bible, © the Lockman Foundation, 1960, 1962, 1963, 1968, 1971, 1972, 1973, 1975, 1977, 1995. Other versions cited are used by permission; NIV, the Holy Bible, New International Version, copyright © 1973, 1978, 1984 by International Bible Society; NRSV, the *New Revised Standard Version of the Bible*, copyright © 1989 by the Division of Christian Education of the National Council of Churches of Christ in the United States of America, all rights reserved; TLB, *The Living Bible* copyright © 1971 by Tyndale House Publishers, Wheaton, Illinois; NKJV, the *New King James Version* copyright © 1979, 1980, 1982, Thomas Nelson, Inc., Publishers. Scripture quotations marked KJV are from *The King James Bible*.

Library of Congress Cataloging-in-Publication Data

Maddox, Sarah, 1938–
    A mother's garden of prayer : cultivating a lifestyle of prayer for your children
      p. cm.
    ISBN 0-8054-1768-0
    1. Mothers—Prayer-books and devotions—English. 2. Grandmothers—Prayer-books
and devotions—English. 3. Children—Religious life. 4. Grandchildren—Religious life.
I. Webb, Patti, 1940– . II. Title.
BV4847.M26   1999
242'.8431—dc21

                                          98-31067
                                             CIP

3 4 5 03 02 01 00 99

SARAH'S DEDICATION

I dedicate this book to my loving mother, Mabel Riley Odle (Mrs. Joe T.), one of the greatest prayer warriors I have ever known. She was the first to challenge and encourage me to pray daily for my children.

I dedicate this book to my precious children and grandchildren: Melanie and Randy Redd, Riley and Emily; Alan and Evie Maddox and Chelsea. It is my joy to intercede for them each day in my garden of prayer.

I dedicate this book to my wonderful husband, Roland, who so lovingly supported, encouraged, and prayed for me all the way through the development of this book.

I dedicate this book to all those precious women who, as a part of my prayer groups, have joined me in praying for my children and grandchildren. They have been a blessing in my life.

PATTI'S DEDICATION

I dedicate this book to my loving husband, Henry, who constantly encourages me to become all that God wants me to be. A special thanks to Henry for giving his unselfish time to help edit *A Mother's Garden of Prayer*.

The prayers in this book are dedicated to my sons, their wives, and my grandchildren: Craig and Barbara Webb, their sons Aaron and Carl; Chuck and Diane Webb, and their daughters Bethany and Myrissa. I am grateful for the love and support they have given me as I have communicated what God is constantly teaching me about praying Scriptures for them.

CONTENTS

THE BEAUTIFUL GARDEN OF PRAYER

By Eleanor Allen Schroll and J. H. Fillmore

There's a garden where Jesus is waiting,
There's a place that is wondrously fair;
For it glows with the light of His presence,
'Tis the beautiful garden of prayer.

There's a garden where Jesus is waiting,
And I go with my burden and care,
Just to learn from His lips words of comfort,
In the beautiful garden of prayer.

There's a garden where Jesus is waiting,
And He bids you to come meet Him there,
Just to walk and to talk with my Saviour,
In the beautiful garden of prayer.

Refrain
O the beautiful garden, the garden of prayer,
O the beautiful garden of prayer;
There my Saviour awaits, and He opens the gates
To the beautiful garden of prayer.

INTRODUCTION

(Sarah) Not many years after I married Roland Maddox, God gave us two precious children. It was my mother, Mabel Odle, who impressed upon my heart the importance of praying for my young children. She urged me to pray for them *each day* in my quiet time with the Lord and as needed throughout the day. She also encouraged me to find other mothers who would join me in intercessory prayer for our precious little ones.

Following her advice, I began to pray daily for my children. I soon found myself praying Scriptures and claiming promises for them. Many times I would write the date and their initials by the verses I prayed.

I also began to pray that God would send me prayer partners. He answered my prayers when several of us young mothers in Memphis, Tennessee, began meeting weekly to intercede for our children. Through the years, the faces in my prayer groups have changed, but the earnestness of the prayers has not. What a joy and blessing those godly prayer partners have been to me, as well as to my children!

When my children were young, I prayed for them as they dealt with peer pressure and challenges in their schoolwork. I stood in the gap for them as they participated in school and church activities. Their spiritual development was at the top of my prayer list. Their physical, mental, and emotional protection were constantly a part of my prayers for them. It didn't take long for our kids to learn that their momma believed in praying about everything!

Many times, as teenagers and young adults, my children have called to request prayer in crisis situations; many times they have asked me to pray as they faced decisions—both major and not so major. I've prayed for them in person and over the phone. As they became adults, I could not "fix" things for them—but I could always stand in the gap for them. No matter where they might be, they knew I *could* pray for them. No matter the circumstances, they knew I *would* pray for them.

Often as I have prayed, a prayer from the Bible has come to mind and I would pray it back to my heavenly Father. At other times, I would hurry to His Word and seek until I could find an appropriate passage to pray back to the Lord on their behalf. Always, the goal of praying for my daughter and son has been that each would become a godly person—one whose life would be fully committed to the Lord Jesus Christ. What a joy it has been to watch their spiritual growth and development through all these years!

I truly believe that praying for my children and grandchildren is a vital, even *necessary,* part of my life as a Christian mother and grand-mother. God has been so faithful to hear and answer my prayers. Sometimes He has answered "Yes," sometimes "No," and at other times, "Wait awhile." But He has never failed me or forsaken me! Our God is utterly trustworthy!

(Patti) God gives me a burden to pray for my children, but I face these barriers:

- I have predetermined ideas of what I want for my children.
- I want to tell God how to solve their problems.
- I want to tell God how to change them.

My husband, Henry, and I have always prayed for our children. I prayed for them before they were born, for their salvation, their mates, their choice of friends, their teachers—all areas of their lives. Some years ago I began to pray specific Scriptures for them. It changes me each time I experience the power of God as I speak Scriptures in prayer. The Lord teaches me to let Him be the problem solver, the change maker. My task is to pray. I've learned that when I pray Scripture, I know I am praying what God desires. I am praying in God's will. I also find that when I search for Scriptures that deal with different issues my children face, God teaches me more about His character and His desire for me, His child. As I pray Scripture, God reveals new insights into how to intercede for others. I may have in my mind a certain solution to a situation facing our family. When I pray Scripture, I find I am again agreeing with God that godly character is most important, not a particular solution I might desire. Whatever the circumstances, I rejoice as I watch God mold my children.

It is important to encourage my sons, daughters-in-love, and grandchildren. Therefore, I often write letters of encouragement to them telling them the Scriptures I have felt led to pray on their behalf. Each has shared with me how much this means to them as they face the daily challenges of raising a family.

(Sarah and Patti) Through the years as mothers and grandmothers God has taught us so much in His "school of prayer." Among the many truths about prayer which have been written on our hearts, are these:

- Pray without ceasing; in everything give thanks; for this is God's will for you in Christ Jesus (1 Thessalonians 5:17–18).
- Let us then approach the throne of grace with confidence, so that we may receive mercy and find grace to help us in our time of need (Hebrews 4:16, NIV).

- Do not be anxious about anything, but in everything, by prayer and petition, with thanksgiving, present your requests to God. And the peace of God, which transcends all understanding, will guard your hearts and your minds in Christ Jesus (Philippians 4:6–7, NIV).
- Ah, Sovereign Lord, you have made the heavens and the earth by your great power and outstretched arm. Nothing is too hard for you (Jeremiah 32:17, NIV).

In Jeremiah 33:3 our heavenly Father lovingly invites us: *Call to me, and I will answer you, and I will tell you great and mighty things, which you do not know.*

May our Lord do many new things in your life and in the lives of your children as you boldly stand in the gap and intercede for them.

In this book, we have called our place of prayer a "prayer garden." As you spend time with the Lord in your prayer garden, may God richly bless you and your children. As you intercede for them, we pray in the words of the prophet Isaiah that:

God will pour out His spirit on your offspring, and His blessing on your descendants. They will spring up among the grass like poplars by streams of water. This one will say, "I am the Lord's;" and they will call on the name of Jacob, and another will write on his hand, "belonging to the Lord" (Isaiah 44:3–5). *In the precious name of Jesus, amen.*

HOW TO USE THIS BOOK

We have designed this book to guide you in praying for your children in your *private prayer times* as well as in *groups of mothers*. Whenever we use "children" and "mothers," you can insert the words "grandchildren" and "grandmothers," if appropriate. Of course, fathers and grandfathers can also use this book.

Every chapter contains Scriptures and sample prayers to use in interceding for your children as they face life's challenges. We have tried to address every area of a child's life from beginning to end.

In most instances the Scripture reference will be printed in its entirety. A sample prayer of paraphrased Scripture will follow the reference(s). We have used "he" in some prayers and "she" in others.

Please take each prayer and personalize it for your own child, thereby making it your personal prayer to God. We encourage you to make the prayers as personal as possible for your own needs.

We believe all prayers for our children and grandchildren should follow these principles:

- They must be offered in the name of Jesus Christ, our Lord.
- They must be based on his Holy Word, the Bible.
- They must be in accordance with His will.
- They must be offered for the purpose of glorifying God.

WHEN TO USE THIS BOOK

FOR PRIVATE PRAYER

In your private prayer times, use this book as a resource:

1. To pray daily prayers for your child.
2. To pray for specific needs that arise.
3. To pray for the development of character qualities or spiritual growth.
4. To guide you in offering your praises to the Lord.

FOR PRAYER GROUPS

In prayer groups, use this book to address a specific request. For example, a mother might give a request to pray for her child who is dealing with a stronghold.

1. Have one member use the verses and prayer for fighting strongholds on page 47.
2. Have another person use the applicable verses and prayers for protection on page 28–38.
3. A third member might use the verses and prayer for the development of a hatred of evil on page 34.
4. Use any others that apply.

ON SPECIAL OCCASIONS

On special occasions use these prayers to bless your child. For example, on your child's graduation day paraphrase the suggested

Scriptures on page 89 into a prayer to be prayed at the family's celebration dinner or party. Give him a framed copy as a permanent keepsake.

The following flowers will be used to illustrate the varied aspects of a child's life on which we need to focus our prayers:

Nasturtium: Individuality
Rose: Love
Camellia: Maturity
Carnation: Courage
Poppy: Peace
Forget-Me-Not: Constancy
Cosmos: Aspiration
Petunia: Happiness
Sunflower: Reverence
Chrysanthemum: Thankfulness

NASTURTIUM

Individuality

NASTURTIUM
Individuality

"*Individual* . . . [is] . . . the nasturtium's heart message . . . In formation, texture, odor, and even coloring it seems to stand alone. . . . Surely, from its individuality springs the nasturtium's true beauty. . . . It is satisfied to be itself. It never seeks to copy the hue or texture of another blossom. . . . It seems to believe that in God's plan it has a particular place, a special mission in being itself at its best. . . . The nasturtium blesses whatever it touches by being itself—individual."[1]

CHAPTER 1
PRAYERS FOR MY UNBORN CHILD

He has blessed your sons within you. Psalm 147:13b

From the moment a mother knows she is expecting a baby, she can begin to intercede for the precious life in her womb. God has designed this little individual as a special gift to his parents. What a joy it will be to pray for this baby's growth and development in the months before his birth.

> For you created my inmost being; you knit me
>   together in my mother's womb.
> I praise you because I am fearfully
>   and wonderfully made;
>   your works are wonderful,
>   I know that full well.
> My frame was not hidden from you when I was
>   made in the secret place.
> When I was woven together in the depths of the
>   earth, your eyes saw my unformed body.
> All the days ordained for me were written in your
>   book before one of them came to be.
>   Psalm 139:13–16 (NIV)

PRAYER: *Lord, You formed my baby's inmost parts; You have skillfully woven this baby in my womb. I give thanks to You, for my baby is fearfully and wonderfully made. Your works are wonderful, and my soul knows it very well. My baby's frame was not hidden from You when You made* _____ *in secret, in the depths of the earth. Your eyes have seen his unformed body; and in*

Your book were written all the days that You plan for him, when my child has not lived one of them. In Jesus' name, amen.

> How precious to me are your thoughts, O God!
> How vast is the sum of them! Psalm 139:17 (NIV)

PRAYER: *How precious are Your thoughts to our baby, O God! Thank You, O Father, for this precious gift of life within me. In Jesus' name, amen.*

> Behold, children are a gift of the Lord;
> The fruit of the womb is a reward.
> Like arrows in the hand of a warrior,
> So are the children of one's youth.
> How blessed is the man whose quiver is full of them;
> They shall not be ashamed,
> When they speak with their enemies in the gate.
>   Psalm 127:3–5

And Jesus increased in wisdom and stature, and in favor with God and man. Luke 2:52 (KJV)

PRAYER: *O Lord, this child You are giving me is a gift from You— she is a unique individual, not like any other. I thank You and praise You for this "arrow in my quiver." I am so blessed to have the privilege of being her mother. Thank You, dear God, for rewarding me in this way.*

May this "arrow" of mine shoot straight and follow Your paths all the days of her life. May she increase in wisdom and stature and in favor with You and others. Oh God, please bless this child within me. In Jesus' name I pray, amen.

ROSE
Love

ROSE

Love

And now abideth faith, hope, and love, these three; but the greatest of these is love (1 Corinthians 13:13).

The rose continually breathes out the marvelous grace of God, "for it is the universal message and messenger of love. . . ." What a fitting symbol this God-given thing of beauty is, not only to represent our love for God and His great love for us, but also "our love for one another."[2]

God has designed each of us to become a thing of beauty on this earth to "be conformed to the likeness of His Son" (Romans 8:29, NIV). Because He loves us so much, we can fully trust Him to work in our lives for our good and His glory.

CHAPTER 2
PRAYERS FOR MY CHILD'S MAJOR DECISIONS

Trust in the Lord with all your heart,
And lean not on your own understanding;
In all your ways acknowledge Him,
And He shall direct your paths.
Proverbs 3:5–6 (NKJV)

Our children are faced with major decisions as they pursue their life's goals. Our loving God has designed a special blueprint for their lives. One of the greatest ways in which we, as mothers, can show our love for our children is to intercede for them as they seek to understand God's will. Our prayers for them will play a vital role both in their decision-making process and in their future success.

DAILY PRAYER TO PRAY FOR YOUR CHILDREN: Paraphrasing the prayer from Colossians 1:9–12 (NIV): *I ask, oh God, that You will fill _____ with the knowledge of Your will through all spiritual wisdom and understanding. I pray this in order that _____ may live a life worthy of You, Lord, and please You in every way: bearing fruit in every good work, growing in the knowledge of God, being strengthened with all power according to Your glorious might. I ask that he might have great endurance and patience, joyfully giving thanks to You, our Father, who has qualified him to share in the inheritance of the saints in the kingdom of light. In Jesus' name, amen.*

SCHOOL CHOICE

I will instruct you and teach you in the way which
  you should go;
I will counsel you with My eye upon you.
  Psalm 32:8

" 'For I know the plans that I have for you,' declares the Lord, 'plans for welfare and not for calamity to give you a future and a hope. Then you will call upon Me and come and pray to Me, and I will listen to you. And you will seek Me and find *Me* when you search for Me with all your heart. And I will be found by you,' declares the Lord." Jeremiah 29:11–14a

PRAYER: *Oh, Heavenly Father, You know the plans that You have for my child. Because of Your great love for him, they will be plans for his welfare to give him a future and a hope. You have said that if we will seek You with all our hearts, we will find You. With all my heart I seek Your will for my child in this choice of schools for him. I look to You to instruct us in the way in which we should go, knowing that You will direct us to the school that will be the very best for him. Thank You, dear Lord. In the name of Jesus, amen.*

CAREER OR JOB CHOICE

I will instruct you and teach you in the way you
  should go;
I will counsel you and watch over you.
  Psalm 32:8 (NIV)

"For I know the plans I have for you," declares the LORD, "plans to prosper you and not to harm you, plans to give you hope and a future. Then you will call upon me and come and pray to me, and I will listen to you. You will seek me and find me when you seek me with all your heart. I will be found by you," declares the Lord. Jeremiah 29:11–14a (NIV)

But seek first His kingdom and His righteousness, and all these things shall be added to you. Matthew 6:33

> The mind of man plans his way,
> But the LORD directs his steps.
>   Proverbs 16:9

For this reason since the day we heard about you, we have not stopped praying for you and asking God to fill you with the knowledge of his will through all spiritual wisdom and understanding. And we pray this in order that you may live a life worthy of the Lord and may please him in every way. Colossians 1:9–10a (NIV)

Always wrestling in prayer for you, that you may stand firm in all the will of God, mature and fully assured. Colossians 4:12b (NIV)

PRAYER: *Oh Lord, I come to You praying that* _____
will seek You with all her heart concerning her career (or job) choice. I pray that she will not make this decision simply with human reasoning, but will look to You to direct her steps. I know that You have special plans just for her that will be for her welfare and not her calamity. How I praise You for that. I pray that she will seek Your

will with all her heart, having the full assurance that You will instruct her in the way she should go and guide her with Your eye.

I pray that she will be filled with the knowledge of Your will in all wisdom and spiritual understanding so that she may walk in a manner worthy of the Lord, to please You in all respects. I will continue to pray earnestly for her, that she will know Your will and stand firm in that knowledge, fully assured of what You desire for her. In Jesus' name, amen.

MINISTRY CHOICE

By this is My Father glorified, that you bear much fruit, and so prove to be My disciples. John 15:8

> Yet I am always with you;
>   you hold me by my right hand.
> You guide me with your counsel.
>   Psalm 73:23–24a (NIV)

Each one should use whatever gift he has received to serve others, faithfully administering God's grace in its various forms. If anyone speaks, he should do it as one speaking the very words of God. If anyone serves, he should do it with the strength God provides, so that in all things God may be praised through Jesus Christ. 1 Peter 4:10–11a (NIV)

And pray for us, too, that God may open a door for our message so that we may proclaim the mystery of Christ, for which I am in chains. Colossians 4:3 (NIV)

To this end also we pray for you always, that our God may count you worthy of your calling, and fulfill every desire for goodness and the work of faith with power. 2 Thessalonians 1:11

PRAYER: *Lord, we know that You are glorified when we bear fruit. I do so desire that my child be engaged in the ministry You have planned for him and bear much fruit for You. Thank You for equipping him with unique gifts to serve others.*

I pray that You will open a door for his ministry that he may proclaim the good news of the gospel of Jesus Christ. Thank You that You, Oh Lord, hold him by the right hand and will guide him with Your counsel to this good work for You. May he always look to You to provide the strength he needs so that in all these things You may be praised through Jesus Christ.

May You, O God, count him worthy of his calling and by Your power may he fulfill every good purpose of Yours. In Jesus' name I pray, amen.

CHOICE OF FRIENDS

But there is a friend who sticks closer than a brother.
    Proverbs 18:24b

A friend loves at all times,
And a brother is born for adversity.
    Proverbs 17:17

Iron sharpens iron,
So one man sharpens another.
    Proverbs 27:17

Don't copy the behavior and customs of this world.
Romans 12:2 (TLB)

> Do not enter the path of the wicked,
> And do not proceed in the way of evil men.
> Proverbs 4:14

But now I am writing you that you must not associate with anyone who calls himself a brother but is sexually immoral or greedy, an idolater or a slanderer, a drunkard or a swindler. With such a man do not even eat. 1 Corinthians 5:11 (NIV)

> Do not make friends with a hot-tempered man,
> do not associate with one easily angered,
> or you may learn his ways
> and get yourself ensnared.
> Proverbs 22:24–25 (NIV)

PRAYER: *Dear Lord, I want to pray for my child in her choice of friends. Please help her to choose the right kind of friends. May each friend be one who will "stick closer than a brother" and be a loving friend at all times.*

May she choose friends who will make her a better and stronger person for associating with them. Please keep her from those who would lead her astray. May she be so strong in her convictions that she can withstand peer pressure. May she choose to follow Your leading instead of copying the behavior and customs of this world. In Jesus' name I pray, amen.

MATE OF GOD'S CHOICE

"'For I know the plans that I have for you,' declares the Lord, 'plans for welfare and not for calamity to give you a future and a hope. Then you will call upon Me and come and pray to Me, and I will listen to you. And you will seek Me and find Me when you search for Me with all your heart. And I will be found by you,' declares the Lord." Jeremiah 29:11–14a

"Haven't you read," he replied, "that at the beginning the Creator 'made them male and female,' and said, 'For this reason a man will leave his father and mother and be united to his wife, and the two will become one flesh'? So they are no longer two, but one. Therefore what God has joined together, let man not separate." Matthew 19:4–6 (NIV)

Do not be yoked together with unbelievers. For what do righteousness and wickedness have in common? . . . What does a believer have in common with an unbeliever? 2 Corinthians 6:14–15 (NIV)

Flee sexual immorality. Every sin that a man does is outside the body, but he who commits sexual immorality sins against his own body. Or do you not know that your body is the temple of the Holy Spirit who is in you, whom you have from God, and you are not your own? For you were bought at a price; therefore glorify God in your body and in your spirit, which are God's. 1 Corinthians 6:18–20 (NKJV)

PRAYER: *Oh Lord, I am coming to You to pray for my child's mate. You know the one You desire for _____ to marry. How*

I pray that he will seek Your will in this very important decision. May he find it and follow it, is my earnest prayer. I pray that he will realize that he is not to be "yoked together with an unbeliever."

When my child finds that person he desires to be his helpmeet, please reveal Your will concerning marriage to him and the one he has chosen in order that they both will know You are joining them together. And please, O Lord, keep them both pure until marriage. In Jesus' precious name I pray, amen.

MY SON'S FUTURE WIFE

A prudent wife is from the Lord.
Proverbs 19:14b (NIV)

A wife of noble character is her husband's crown,
but a disgraceful wife is like decay in his bones.
Proverbs 12:4 (NIV)

The heart of her husband trusts in her,
And he will have no lack of gain.
She does him good and not evil
All the days of her life.
Proverbs 31:11–12

Wives, be subject to your own husbands, as to the Lord. Ephesians 5:22

Then they can train the younger women to love their husbands and children, to be self-controlled and pure, to be busy at home, to be kind, and to be subject to their husbands, so that no one will malign the word of God. Titus 2:4–5 (NIV)

PRAYER: *Dear Lord, I desire that my son find a prudent wife—one who will be of noble character—a virtuous woman. I pray that she will truly love my son above all others and will be completely trustworthy. Oh, Lord, may she have the desire to do him good and not evil all of his life. I also pray that she will love her husband and her children, that she will be self-controlled, pure and kind, and willing to be subject to her husband.*

I pray that my son and his wife will leave their parents and be united to each other as long as they both shall live. And, O Lord, I pray that what You have joined together, no one will ever separate. In Jesus' name, amen.

MY DAUGHTER'S FUTURE HUSBAND

A foolish son is his father's ruin.
Proverbs 19:13a (NIV)

Husbands, love your wives, just as Christ loved the church and gave himself up for her. . . . Husbands ought to love their own wives as their own bodies. Ephesians 5:25, 28 (NIV)

Likewise urge the young men to be sensible; in all things show yourself to be an example of good deeds, with purity in doctrine, dignified, sound in speech which is beyond reproach, in order that the opponent may be put to shame, having nothing bad to say about us. Titus 2:6–8

"'For this reason a man will leave his father and mother and be united to his wife, and the two will become one flesh.' . . . So they are no longer two, but one. Therefore what God has joined together, let man not separate." Matthew 19:5–6 (NIV)

PRAYER: *Dear Lord, I desire that my daughter find a husband who is not a foolish man, but a wise one. I pray that he will be one who will love her as Christ loved the church and gave Himself for it. I pray also that her husband will love her as he loves himself. I pray that he will be sensible and in all things show himself to be an example of good deeds, doctrinal purity, dignity, and speech which is beyond reproach.*

I pray that my daughter and her husband will leave their parents and be united to each other as long as they both shall live. And, O Lord, I pray that what You have joined together, no one will ever separate. In Jesus' name, amen.

CAMELLIA

Maturity

CAMELLIA
Maturity

The message of the camellia is of a "heart's yearning and that yearning is for *perfection,* that completion in growth which the Master had in mind when he urged his disciples to strive to be perfect just as his Father was perfect—to reach full stature spiritually. . . . This is no mushroom growth but the slow, laborious march of the child of God toward spiritual adulthood. It requires the hand of time; but in the end it will be like the shining light 'that shineth more and more unto the perfect day' (Proverbs 4:18, KJV)."[3]

CHAPTER 3
PRAYERS FOR MY CHILD'S SPIRITUAL GROWTH

But grow in the grace and knowledge of our Lord
and Savior Jesus Christ. 2 Peter 3:18

The goal of all our praying for our children ought to be that they become godly young men and women. This will materialize as they progress in their spiritual growth. Because this development has many aspects, we have included a broad range of prayers to cover the diverse stages of growth. We begin with a prayer for the child's salvation, a prerequisite to spiritual growth.

PRAYERS FOR MY CHILD'S SALVATION

God, our Savior who wants all men to be saved and to come to the knowledge of the truth. 1 Timothy 2:3b–4 (NIV)

For all have sinned and fall short of the glory of God. Romans 3:23

But God demonstrates His own love toward us, in that while we were yet sinners, Christ died for us. Romans 5:8

For the wages of sin is death, but the free gift of God is eternal life in Jesus Christ our Lord. Romans 6:23

If you confess with your mouth Jesus as Lord, and believe in your heart that God raised Him from the dead, you shall be saved. Romans 10:9–10

Then Jesus told his disciples a parable to show them that they should always pray and not give up. Luke 18:1 (NIV)

Pray continually. 1 Thessalonians 5:17 (NIV)

PRAYER: *Oh dear Lord, I know that You desire for all people to be saved and to come to know You as Savior and Lord. I pray that my child will come to the realization that he is a sinner in need of a Savior. I pray that he will repent of his sin, believe in his heart that Jesus died on the cross to save him, and receive Jesus into his heart as his Savior and Lord, thereby receiving the gift of eternal life.*

May he be saved at an early age so that he can serve You all his life. But Lord, no matter how long it takes, I shall pray without ceasing until he makes this most important decision of his life, knowing that I should never stop interceding for him. In Jesus' name I pray, amen.

GENERAL PRAYERS FOR SPIRITUAL GROWTH

I keep asking that the God of our Lord Jesus Christ, the glorious Father, may give you the Spirit of wisdom and revelation, so that you may know him better. I pray also that the eyes of your heart may be enlightened in order that you may know the hope to which he has called you, the riches of his glorious inheritance in the saints, and his incomparably great power for us who believe. That power is like the working of his mighty strength, which he exerted in Christ when he raised him from the dead and seated him at his right hand in the heavenly realms. Ephesians 1:17–20 (NIV)

PRAYER: *Oh God of our Lord Jesus Christ, give my child the Spirit of wisdom and revelation so that she may know You better. Enlighten the eyes of her heart in order that she may know the hope to which You have called her, the riches of Your glorious inheritance in the saints, and Your incomparably great power for her because she believes. Help her to realize that that power is like the working of Your mighty strength, which You exerted in Christ when You raised Him from the dead. In Jesus' name, amen.*

I pray that out of his glorious riches he may strengthen you with power through his Spirit in your inner being, so that Christ may dwell in your hearts through faith. And I pray that you, being rooted and established in love, may have power, together with all the saints, to grasp how wide and long and high and deep is the love of Christ, and to know this love that surpasses knowledge—that you may be filled to the measure of all the fullness of God. Ephesians 3:16–19 (NIV)

PRAYER: *I pray that out of Your glorious riches You will strengthen _____ with Your power through Your Spirit in his inner being, so that You may dwell in his heart through faith. And I pray that he, being rooted and established in love, may have power, together with all the saints, to grasp how wide and long and high and*

deep is Your love. I ask that he will know that this love surpasses knowledge. I also ask that he will be filled with Your fullness. In Jesus' name, amen.

PRAYERS FOR A HEAVENLY MIND-SET

Since, then, you have been raised with Christ, set your hearts on things above, where Christ is seated at the right hand of God. Set your minds on things above, not on earthly things. Colossians 3:1–2 (NIV)

Surely you heard of him and were taught in him in accordance with the truth that is in Jesus. You were taught, with regard to your former way of life, to put off your old self, which is being corrupted by its deceitful desires; to be made new in the attitude of your minds; and to put on the new self, created to be like God in true righteousness and holiness. Ephesians 4:21–24 (NIV)

Do not conform any longer to the pattern of this world, but be transformed by the renewing of your mind. Then you will be able to test and approve what God's will is—his good, pleasing and perfect will. Romans 12:2 (NIV)

Jesus replied: "'Love the Lord your God with all your heart and with all your soul and with all your mind.'" Matthew 22:37 (NIV)

PRAYER: *Dear God, teach my child to love You with all her mind. May she choose to set her mind on things above—not on earthly things but on what the Holy Spirit desires. Help her to learn not to*

conform to the pattern of this world, but to be transformed by the renewing of her mind. Father, help her put off any old habits that are ungodly and destructive. May she daily be made new in the attitude of her mind by constantly letting You change her attitudes and thoughts for the better. In Jesus' name, amen.

PRAYERS FOR SUBMISSION TO AUTHORITY

OBEDIENCE TO PARENTS

Children, obey your parents in the Lord, for this is right. "Honor your father and mother"—which is the first commandment with a promise— "that it may go well with you and that you may enjoy long life on the earth." Fathers, do not exasperate your children; instead, bring them up in the training and instruction of the Lord. Ephesians 6:1–4 (NIV)

Children, be obedient to your parents in all things, for this is well-pleasing to the Lord. Colossians 3:20

> My son, observe the commandment of your father,
>   And do not forsake the teaching of your mother.
>   Proverbs 6:20

> Listen, my sons, to a father's instruction;
>   pay attention and gain understanding.
> I give you sound learning,
>   so do not forsake my teaching.
>   Proverbs 4:1 (NIV)

PRAYER FOR A YOUNG CHILD: *Lord, I so want my little one to obey me. I realize that I must model Your character before my child and not exasperate her. Teach me how to bring her up in the training and instruction that models You. Show me how to teach her obedience that it may go well with her. Show me how to teach her to listen to my words, to pay attention and gain understanding of Your teachings. In Your name I pray, amen.*

PRAYER FOR OLDER TEEN-AGERS OR YOUNG ADULTS: *Oh Lord, I pray that my children will obey their parents as long as they are under our authority. When they leave home, I pray that they will continue to observe the commandments and teachings we have imparted to them all their growing up years. May they honor their parents all the days of their lives so that it may go well with them. In Jesus' name I pray, amen.*

OBEDIENCE TO OTHER AUTHORITIES

Let every person be in subjection to the governing authorities. For there is no authority except from God, and those which exist are established by God. Therefore whoever resists authority has opposed the ordinance of God; and they who have opposed will receive condemnation upon themselves. Romans 13:1

Submit yourselves for the Lord's sake to every human institution, whether to a king as the one in authority, or to governors as sent by him for the punishment of evildoers and the praise of those who do right. For such is the will of God that by doing right you may silence the ignorance of foolish men. 1 Peter 2:13

Servants, be submissive to your masters with all respect, not only to those who are good and gentle, but also to those who are unreasonable. 1 Peter 2:18

PRAYER: *Dear Lord, I pray that my child will learn early to respect authority and to obey those who have authority over him. Help him not to be rebellious and self-willed, but respectful of his superiors. May he realize the importance of doing right, even when those in charge are being unreasonable. In Jesus' name, amen.*

OBEDIENCE TO GOD

We must obey God rather than men. Acts 5:29

That you may obey Jesus Christ and be sprinkled with His blood. 1 Peter 1:2b

Then Jesus said to His disciples, "If anyone wishes to come after Me, let him deny himself and take up his cross, and follow Me. For whoever wishes to save his life shall lose it; but whoever loses his life for My sake shall find it." Matthew 16:24

PRAYER: *Dear Heavenly Father, I pray that my child might be obedient to You by receiving Jesus Christ as his Savior and Lord. If ever she has to choose between God and man, may she have the spiritual strength to obey You, instead of man. May she realize that to obey Jesus fully is to deny herself, take up her cross, and follow Him. I pray that in the days ahead, she will be willing to do just that. In Your name I pray, amen.*

PRAYERS FOR GOD TO WORK IN MY CHILD'S LIFE

May the God of peace, who through the blood of the eternal covenant brought back from the dead our Lord Jesus, that great Shepherd of the sheep, equip you with everything good for doing his will, and may he work in us what is pleasing to him, through Jesus Christ, to whom be glory for ever and ever, amen. Hebrews 13:20–21 (NIV)

Being confident of this, that he who began a good work in you will carry it on to completion until the day of Christ Jesus. Philippians 1:6 (NIV)

For it is God who is at work in you, both to will and to work for His good pleasure. Philippians 2:13

Until we all attain to the unity of the faith, and of the knowledge of the Son of God, to a mature man, to the measure of the stature which belongs to the fullness of Christ. Ephesians 4:13

PRAYER: *Dear God, I am so grateful that You began a good work in my child on the day of his salvation, and will carry it on to completion until the day Jesus comes again. Thank You for equipping him with everything he needs to do Your will. Please work in him to accomplish Your good pleasure so that he will become spiritually mature. In Jesus' name, amen.*

CARNATION

Courage

CARNATION

Courage

"Courage is the thought emanating from [the carnation's] lovely heart and pervading the very air it breathes. . . . Who can number the sick, the sorrowing, the lonely of heart who have received strength from its word of *courage*. . . . It endures so well, standing erect, proud, and fragrant for days. To the suffering one it says, 'Only be thou strong and very courageous' (Joshua 1:7, KJV).

"Through the power of the Creator . . . Redeemer and Lord, . . . [we can] conquer in the name of him who said, 'Be of good cheer; I have overcome the world' (John 16:33, KJV)."[4]

CHAPTER 4
PRAYERS FOR MY
CHILD'S PROTECTION

Arise, cry aloud in the night
At the beginning of the night watches;
Pour out your heart like water
Before the presence of the Lord;
Lift up your hands to Him
For the life of your little ones.
Lamentations 2:19

We need to cry aloud to our heavenly Father for the lives of our children. Our daily prayers for them need to include prayers for their protection: physical, mental, emotional, and spiritual. We should also pray that they will continually look to the Lord for courage and strength.

PHYSICAL PROTECTION

The angel of the Lord encamps around
   them who fear Him,
And rescues them.
   Psalm 34:7

The Lord is my light and my salvation;
Whom shall I fear?
The Lord is the defense of my life;
Whom shall I dread?
   Psalm 27:1

> For he will command his angels concerning you
>> to guard you in all your ways;
> they will lift you up in their hands,
>> so that you will not strike your foot against a stone.
>> Psalm 91:11–12 (NIV)

> Do not be afraid of sudden fear,
> Nor of the onslaught of the wicked when it comes;
> For the Lord will be your confidence,
> And will keep your foot from being caught.
>> Proverbs 3:25–26

And pray that we may be delivered from wicked and evil men, for not everyone has faith. But the Lord is faithful, and he will strengthen and protect you from the evil one. 2 Thessalonians 3:2–3 (NIV)

PRAYER: *Oh Lord, in this evil day in which we live, I cry out to You for the life of my child! I pray for his physical protection today. I thank You, dear Lord, that You command Your angels concerning us to guard us in all our ways. What a comfort that is to me.*

I pray that _____ may be delivered from wicked and evil men today. Please protect him from attack, abuse, abduction, and addiction. When he is afraid, may he look to You to be his confidence. In the strong name of Jesus, amen.

MENTAL PROTECTION

> For as he thinks within himself, so he is.
>> Proverbs 23:7

Finally, brethren, whatever is true, whatever is honorable, whatever is right, whatever is pure, whatever is lovely, whatever is of good repute, if there is any excellence and if anything worthy of praise, let your mind dwell on these things. Philippians 4:8

> I meditate on your precepts and consider your ways.
>   Psalm 119:15 (NIV)

As a result, we are no longer to be children, tossed here and there by waves, and carried about by every wind of doctrine, by the trickery of men, by craftiness in deceitful scheming. Ephesians 4:14

But if any of you lacks wisdom, let him ask of God. James 1:5

For the weapons of our warfare are not of the flesh, but divinely powerful for the destruction of fortresses. We are destroying speculations and every lofty thing raised up against the knowledge of God, and we are taking every thought captive to the obedience of Christ. 2 Corinthians 10:4–5

> I have hidden your word in my heart that I might
>   not sin against you.
>   Psalm 119:11 (NIV)

PRAYER: *Oh God, I pray that You will protect my child's mind, knowing that she will be what she thinks within herself. I pray that she will meditate on Your precepts and consider Your ways, letting her mind focus on whatever is true, honorable, right, pure, lovely, and good. May she think on these good things and not on lies, or on dishonorable, wrong, impure, unlovely, or evil things. I pray that she will hide Your word in her heart so that she will not sin against You.*

I pray that when she needs wisdom, she will ask You for it. I pray that she will go to Your Word and read it carefully, so that she will not be a double-minded woman and thus unstable. I pray that she will use Your weapons to demolish arguments and every obstacle that sets itself up against Your knowledge. I pray that she will deliberately take captive every thought and make it obedient to Christ.

Lord, keep her from being tossed here and there, and carried about by every wind of doctrine. Do not let her be taken in by the trickery of men or by the craftiness of their deceitful scheming. Only You, dear Lord, can protect her mind in this evil day. How I pray that You will hear my earnest prayer for my child! In Jesus' name, amen.

EMOTIONAL PROTECTION

I have set the Lord continually before me;
    Because He is at my right hand,
    I will not be shaken. Psalm 16:8

Wisdom and knowledge will be the stability
    of your times. Isaiah 33:6 (NKJV)

Be anxious for nothing, but in everything by prayer and supplication with thanksgiving let your requests be made known to God. And the peace of God, which surpasses all comprehension, shall guard your hearts and your minds in Christ Jesus. Philippians 4:6–7

Be strong in the Lord and in the strength of His might. Ephesians 6:10

For God has not given us a spirit of fear, but of power, and of love and of a sound mind. 2 Timothy 1:7 (NKJV)

And the Lord is the One who goes ahead of you; He will be with you. He will not fail you or forsake you. Do not fear, or be dismayed. Deuteronomy 31:8

> When I am afraid,
>> I will put my trust in Thee.
>> Psalm 56:3

PRAYER: *Dearest Lord, I come to You asking You to protect my child in the area of his emotions. I pray that he will seek Your wisdom and will walk by faith, not feelings. Let him come to know You more and more intimately. Help him to learn that Your wisdom and the knowledge of the Lord Jesus Christ will give him stability, no matter what the situation may be.*

Please help _____ to realize that You are always with him. You will never leave him or forsake him. May he know that You have not given him a spirit of fear, but of power, and love and of a sound mind. Oh God, please deliver him from any fears he has. May he face his fears and deal with them through the power of the Holy Spirit. When he is afraid, let him learn to put his trust in You. In Jesus' name, amen.

But the fruit of the Spirit is love, joy, peace, patience, kindness, goodness, faithfulness, gentleness and self-control. Against such things there is no law. Those who belong to Christ Jesus have crucified the sinful nature with its passions and desires. Since we live by the Spirit, let us keep in step with the Spirit. Galatians 5:22 (NIV)

Therefore, as God's chosen people, holy and dearly loved, clothe yourselves with compassion, kindness, humility, gentleness and patience. Bear with each other and forgive whatever grievances you may have against one another. Forgive as the Lord forgave you. Colossians 3:12 (NIV)

PRAYER: *Holy Spirit, teach my child to grow in love, joy, peace, patience, kindness, goodness, faithfulness, gentleness, and self-control. Show him that since he lives by Your Spirit, he can choose to let You control his life. Help him to realize that he is one of Your chosen ones, holy and dearly loved. Show him how to clothe himself with compassion, kindness, humility, gentleness, and patience. Teach him to bear with others and forgive whatever grievances he may have against them. In Jesus' precious name, amen.*

SPIRITUAL PROTECTION

PROTECTION OF HIS HEART

"For God sees not as man sees, for man looks at the outward appearance, but the Lord looks at the heart." 1 Samuel 16:7

> My son, pay attention to what I say;
> listen closely to my words.

Do not let them out of your sight,
   keep them within your heart;
   for they are life to those who find them
   and health to a man's whole body.
Above all else, guard your heart,
   for it is the wellspring of life.
Put away perversity from your mouth;
   keep corrupt talk far from your lips.
Let your eyes look straight ahead,
   fix your gaze directly before you.
Make level paths for your feet
   and take only ways that are firm.
Do not swerve to the right or the left;
   keep your foot from evil.
   Proverbs 4:20–27 (NIV)

Let the words of my mouth and the
   meditation of my heart
Be acceptable in Thy sight,
O Lord, my rock and my Redeemer.
   Psalm 19:14

PRAYER: *God, help my daughter to listen to You and to Your Word. Help her to keep Your words in her heart, for they are life to her and health to her whole body. Show her how to guard her heart, to put away perversity from her mouth, to keep corrupt talk far from her lips, and to let her eyes look straight ahead, walking only in ways that are firm. Keep her from swerving to the right or to the left and keep her feet from evil.*

I pray that the words of her mouth and the meditation of her heart will be acceptable to You, O Lord. In Jesus' name, amen.

DEVELOPMENT OF A HATRED FOR EVIL

Hate evil, you who love the Lord.
　Psalm 97:10

Abhor what is evil; cling to what is good. Romans 12:9b

But examine everything carefully; hold fast to that which is good; abstain from every form of evil. 1 Thessalonians 5:21–22

　Thy word have I treasured in my heart,
　That I might not sin against Thee.
　　Psalm 119:11

Put on the full armor of God, that you may be able to stand firm against the schemes of the devil. Ephesians 6:11

PRAYER: *Oh Lord, I pray that my child will develop a keen sense of what is right and wrong and a strong hatred for that which is evil. I pray that he will examine everything carefully, holding fast to that which is good. May he hide Your word in his heart that he might not sin against You. May he put on Your whole armor so that he will be able to stand firm against the schemes of the devil. Help him to abstain from every form of evil. In Jesus' name, amen.*

DELIVERANCE FROM EVIL AND THE EVIL ONE

"And do not lead us into temptation but deliver us from evil. For Thine is the kingdom, and the power and the glory, forever, Amen." Matthew 6:13

PRAYER: *I pray that You will deliver _____ from evil. In Jesus' name, amen.*

FROM PERVERSE AND EVIL MEN

Finally, brethren, pray for us . . . that we may be delivered from perverse and evil men; for not all have faith. But the Lord is faithful and He will strengthen and protect you from the evil one. 2 Thessalonians 3:1–3

> "To grant us that we, being delivered
>   from the hand of our enemies,
> Might serve Him without fear,
> In holiness and righteousness
>   before Him all our days."
>   Luke 1:74–75

PRAYER: *I pray that _____ will be delivered from perverse and evil men. Lord, I know Your faithfulness and I ask that You will strengthen _____ and protect her from the evil one. Help her to see Your faithfulness. I pray that You will rescue her from the hand of her enemies, so she can always serve You without fear. In the strong name of Jesus, amen.*

From Bondage

With gentleness correcting those who are in opposition, if perhaps God may grant them repentance leading to the knowledge of the truth, and they may come to their senses and escape from the snare of the devil, having been held captive by him to do his will. 2 Timothy 2:25–26

It was for freedom that Christ set us free; therefore keep standing firm and do not be subject again to a yoke of slavery. Galatians 5:1

PRAYER: *Oh heavenly Father, please help my child to repent of his sin, gain a knowledge of Your truth, and come to his senses so that he can escape from the snare of the devil who has been holding him captive. May he then stand firm and not be subject again to this yoke of slavery. In Jesus' name, amen.*

From Satan's Power

You are from God, little children, and have overcome them; because greater is He who is in you than he who is in the world. 1 John 4:4

"And whatever you ask in My name, that will I do, that the Father may be glorified in the Son." John 14:13

And they overcame him because of the blood of the Lamb, and because of the word of their testimony, and they did not love their life even to death. Revelation 12:11

But the Lord is faithful, and He will strengthen and protect you from the evil one. 2 Thessalonians 3:3

Establish my footsteps in Thy word,
  And do not let any iniquity have
  dominion over me. Psalm 119:133

"Deliver us from evil." Matthew 6:13

Have you not put a hedge around him and his household and everything he has? Job 1:10 (NIV)

PRAYER: *Lord God Jehovah, I ask in the name of the Lord Jesus Christ and by the power of His shed blood that You protect my child from Satan, the evil one. You have taught us that Christ is in us and He is greater than Satan, who is in the world. So today I take a stand against Satan in this situation _____ is facing, claiming the overcoming power of the Lord Jesus Christ. I ask that You place a hedge of protection around _____ to protect him from the evil one. In the blessed name of Jesus I pray, amen.*

PROTECTION FROM UNGODLY LIVING

Since, then, you have been raised with Christ, set your hearts on things above, where Christ is seated at the right hand of God. Set your minds on things above, not on earthly things. For you died, and your life is now hidden with Christ in God. When Christ, who is your life, appears, then you also will appear with him in glory.

Put to death, therefore, whatever belongs to your earthly nature: sexual immorality, impurity, lust, evil desires and greed, which is idolatry. Colossians 3:1–5 (NIV)

But now you must rid yourselves of all such things as these: anger, rage, malice, slander, and filthy language from your lips. Do not lie to each other since you have taken off your old self with its practices and have put on the new self, which is being renewed in knowledge in the image of its Creator. Colossians 3:8–10 (NIV)

PRAYER: *Father, protect my child from ungodly living. Show her how to set her heart on Your things and not on earthly things. Help her to see that her life is hidden in You. Show her how to put to death her earthly nature of sexual immorality, impurity, lust, evil desires, and greed.*

Teach her how to rid herself of anger, rage, malice, slander, and filthy language. Show her how not to lie. Help her to know that when she became a Christian, she became a new person and is being renewed in knowledge in Your image, her Creator. In Jesus' name, amen.

POPPY

Peace

POPPY

Peace

"The poppy stands for a peace which the world knows little of but the kind which it must seek if wars are ever to cease. . . . The peace which the poppy symbolizes is one which the smiles of the world cannot bestow; nor can the frowns of the world take it away. It is the peace to which every believing soul is rightful heir because Jesus, his blessed Lord, bequeathed it to him."[5]

Jesus said to those in the upper room and to us: "Peace I leave with you, my peace I give unto you; not as the world giveth give I unto you. Let not your heart be troubled, neither let it be afraid" (John 14: 27, KJV).

CHAPTER 5
PRAYERS FOR MY CHILD UNDER PRESSURE

Be anxious for nothing, but in everything by prayer and supplication with thanksgiving let your requests be made known to God. And the peace of God, which surpasses all comprehension, shall guard your hearts and your minds in Christ Jesus. Philippians 4:6–7

Daily pressures confront my children. It is essential that I intercede for them in the midst of all their trials, so that they may experience the peace which only God can give. No matter how great or how small their problems may seem, I am to "draw near with confidence to the throne of grace, that [my family] may receive mercy and may find grace to help in time of need" (Hebrews 4:16).

FACING TRIALS

SUFFERING FROM AN ILLNESS OR ACCIDENT

Beloved, I pray that in all respects you may prosper and be in good health, just as your soul prospers. 3 John 2

Therefore, confess your sins to one another, and pray for one another, so that you may be healed. The effective prayer of a righteous man can accomplish much. James 5:16

"'For I will restore you to health
And I will heal you of your
wounds,' declares the Lord."
Jeremiah 30:17

Heal me, O Lord, and I will be healed.
Jeremiah 17:14

[God] comforts us in all our troubles, so that we can comfort those in any trouble with the comfort we ourselves have received from God. 2 Corinthians 1:4 (NIV)

PRAYER: *Dear heavenly Father, You have admonished us to confess our sins and pray for the healing of others. I do confess my sins of* _____.

I now call on You out of a pure heart and ask that You restore my child to health; heal her, O Lord. Please comfort her in her affliction that she may be able to comfort others. I pray that she will truly be in good health. In Jesus' precious name I pray, amen.

SUFFERING FROM A LIFELONG ILLNESS

We do not want you to be uninformed, brothers, about the hardships we suffered in the province of Asia. We were under great pressure, far beyond our ability to endure, so that we despaired even of life. Indeed, in our hearts we felt the sentence of death. But this happened that we might not rely on ourselves but on God, who raises the dead. He has delivered us from such a deadly peril, and he will deliver us.

On him we have set our hope that he will continue to deliver us. 2 Corinthians 1:8–10 (NIV)

PRAYER: *Father, God, it is so hard to talk about our child who has been diagnosed with this lifelong debilitating illness. You know my constant desire is for You to heal him. I have the faith; I know You can heal him. Right now, though, he is suffering.*

Father, thank You for these words You inspired Paul to write about the time his suffering was far beyond his ability to endure, so that he despaired even of life. We are feeling this way right now about this illness. Heavenly Father, Paul said he was able to see that his suffering happened so that he might not rely on himself but on You. In the same way, we ask that You would continue to guide us so that during this lifelong illness we might depend on You and Your strength and not on ourselves. In Jesus' name, amen.

SUFFERING CONSEQUENCES OF SIN

My son, do not despise the Lord's discipline
    and do not resent his rebuke,
because the Lord disciplines those he loves,
    as a father the son he delights in.
    Proverbs 3:11–12 (NIV)

Whoever loves discipline loves knowledge,
    but he who hates correction is stupid.
A good man obtains favor from the Lord,
    but the Lord condemns a crafty man.
    Proverbs 12:1–2 (NIV)

Through love and faithfulness sin is atoned for;
    through the fear of the Lord a man avoids evil.
    Proverbs 16:6 (NIV)

The fear of the Lord is the beginning of wisdom,
    and knowledge of the Holy One is understanding.
For through me your days will be many,
    and years will be added to your life.
If you are wise, your wisdom will reward you;
    if you are a mocker, you alone will suffer.
    Proverbs 9:10–12 (NIV)

PRAYER: *My child has sinned, Father. Help him now as he faces the consequences of this sin, not to despise Your discipline and not to resent Your rebuke. Help him to feel Your love and to know that You discipline because You love him. Help him not to hate this correction. Help him to be able to realize Your love and faithfulness because You have forgiven him. Please show him how to fear You so that he can have Your wisdom and avoid evil. In the name of Jesus, amen.*

SUFFERING BECAUSE OF HER CHRISTIAN STAND

However, if you suffer as a Christian, do not be ashamed, but praise God that you bear that name. 1 Peter 4:16 (NIV)

Praise be to the God and Father of our Lord Jesus Christ! In His great mercy He has given us new birth into a living hope through the resurrection of Jesus Christ from the dead, and into an inheritance that can never perish, spoil or fade—kept in heaven for you, who through faith are shielded by God's power until the coming of the salvation that is ready to be revealed in the last time. In this you greatly rejoice, though now for a little while you may have had to suffer grief in all kinds of trials. These have come so that your faith—of greater worth than gold, which perishes even though refined by fire—may be proved genuine and may result in praise, glory and honor when Jesus Christ is revealed. 1 Peter 1:3–7 (NIV)

What, then, shall we say in response to this? If God is for us, who can be against us? He who did not spare his own Son, but gave him up for us all—how will he not also, along with him, graciously give us all things? Who will bring any charge against those whom God has chosen? It is God who justifies. Who is he that condemns? Christ Jesus, who died—more than that, who was raised to life—is at the right hand of God and is also interceding for us. Who shall separate us from the love of Christ? Shall trouble or hardship or persecution or famine or nakedness or danger or sword? . . . No, in all these things we are more than conquerors through him who loved us. For I am convinced that neither death nor life, neither angels nor demons, neither the present nor the future, nor any powers, neither height nor depth, nor anything else in all creation, will be able to separate us from the love of God that is in Christ Jesus our Lord. Romans 8:31–35, 37–39 (NIV)

PRAYER: *Dear God, my daughter is suffering because of her stand for You. I praise You that she bears Your name. Help her to be obedient, to praise You and not be ashamed. You have said she is shielded by faith through Your power. Help her recognize that power. Even*

though she has to suffer grief in all kinds of trials, may she see that they have come so that her faith may be proved genuine and result in praise, glory, and honor when You are revealed. We praise You that when others condemn her, You do not. May she constantly be aware of the wonderful truth that nothing can separate her from Your love. In Jesus' holy and precious name, amen.

FIGHTING STRONGHOLDS IN HIS LIFE

I beg you that when I come I may not have to be as bold as I expect to be toward some people who think that we live by the standards of this world. For though we live in the world, we do not wage war as the world does. The weapons we fight with are not the weapons of the world. On the contrary, they have divine power to demolish strongholds. We demolish arguments and every pretension that sets itself up against the knowledge of God, and we take captive every thought to make it obedient to Christ. 2 Corinthians 10:2 (NIV)

Therefore, behold, I will hedge up her way with thorns, and I will build a wall against her so that she cannot find her paths, and she will pursue her lovers but she will not overtake them; and she will seek them, but will not find them. Hosea 2:6–7a

PRAYER: *Father, right now my son is caught up in a terrible stronghold, but does not realize that he cannot fight this problem as the world does. Help him to see that to tear down strongholds, he must use Your weapons, which have Your power to destroy this evil in his life. Help him also to see that with these weapons, he can tear*

down every argument that is contrary to the knowledge of God. May he learn to take every thought he has, release those thoughts to You, and obey You, O Christ.

I pray that if he seeks after that which is evil today, you will place a hedge of thorns around him so that he will not find this evil. In Jesus' name, amen.

FACING DIFFICULTIES IN MARRIAGE

Now as the church submits to Christ, so also wives should submit to their husbands in everything. Husbands, love your wives, just as Christ loved the church and gave himself up for her. Ephesians 5:24–26 (NIV)

"'For this reason a man will leave his father and mother and be united to his wife, and the two will become one flesh.' . . . So they are no longer two, but one. Therefore what God has joined together, let man not separate." Matthew 19:5–6 (NIV)

PRAYER: *Father, please protect the marriage of our children, _____ and _____. I thank You that You gave them to each other as husband and wife. I ask that You show my son how to love his wife as You loved the church and died for it. Show his wife how to submit to him as to the Lord. May she learn the most effective ways to convey to him how much she loves and respects him. Help me to honor Your instructions in deed, action, and word. Help me to allow my son to "leave" his father and mother and be united to his wife. In Jesus' name, amen.*

STRUGGLING TO PERSEVERE

STRUGGLING TO SURVIVE

"Come to me, all you who are weary and burdened, and I will give you rest." Matthew 11:28 (NIV)

> He gives strength to the weary,
>   And to him who lacks might He increases power.
> Though youths grow weary and tired,
>   And vigorous young men stumble badly,
>   Yet those who wait for the Lord
>   Will gain new strength;
>   They will mount up with wings like eagles,
>   They will run and not get tired,
>   They will walk and not become weary.
>   Isaiah 40:29–31

Consider it pure joy, my brothers, whenever you face trials of many kinds, because you know that the testing of your faith develops perseverance. Perseverance must finish its work so that you may be mature and complete, not lacking anything. If any of you lacks wisdom, he should ask God, who gives generously to all without finding fault, and it will be given to him. James 1:2–5 (NIV)

> The Lord's lovingkindnesses
>   indeed never cease,
> For His compassions never fail.

They are new every morning;
Great is Thy faithfulness.
　　Lamentations 3:22–23

PRAYER: *Father, You know better than anyone how I want to solve all my daughter's problems right now. She is so tired and weary. Show her how to come to You for the rest she so desperately needs. May she ask You for Your strength and power so that she will mount up with wings like an eagle, and will be able to keep on going without running out of steam.*

You told us, loving Father, to consider it pure joy whenever we face trials. Right now I am having trouble doing that, and I know my daughter is too. Help us both to be obedient to You. I know that the testing of my daughter's faith will develop perseverance, and that when it finishes its work, she will be mature and complete, lacking nothing. O God, this is what I desire.

I come to You in praise, with a desire to have pure joy as my daughter faces this trial. I ask for wisdom for her, knowing You are the author and giver of wisdom. Oh, Lord, may she come to understand that Your loving kindness and compassion never cease. They are new every morning. May she look to You for her daily provision. In Jesus' holy and precious name, amen.

STRUGGLING TO FORGIVE

Be kind and compassionate to one another, forgiving each other, just as in Christ God forgave you. Ephesians 4:32 (NIV)

"You have heard that it was said, 'Love your neighbor and hate your enemy.' But I tell you: Love your enemies and pray for those who persecute you, that you may be sons of your Father in heaven. He causes his sun to rise on the evil and the good and sends rain on the righteous and the unrighteous." Matthew 5:43–45 (NIV)

"Forgive us our debts, as we also have forgiven our debtors." Matthew 6:12 (NIV)

PRAYER: *Father, my son is having trouble forgiving his friend for all the hurtful things he has done. Help my son to forgive just as in Christ You forgave him. Help him to love _____ and pray for him. Show me how to model that for him. This is hard, Lord. In Jesus' precious name, I pray, amen.*

STRUGGLING TO KEEP A MARRIAGE INTACT

"Haven't you read," he replied, "that at the beginning the Creator 'made them male and female,' and said, 'For this reason a man will leave his father and mother and be united to his wife, and the two will become one flesh'? So they are no longer two, but one. Therefore what God has joined together, let man not separate." Matthew 19:4–6 (NIV)

Do not be deceived: God cannot be mocked. A man reaps what he sows. The one who sows to please his sinful nature, from that nature will reap destruction; the one who sows to please the Spirit, from the Spirit will reap eternal life. Galatians 6:7–8 (NIV)

Has not the LORD made them one? In flesh and spirit they are his. And why one? Because he was seeking godly offspring. So guard yourself in your spirit, and do not break faith with the wife of your youth.

"I hate divorce," says the LORD God of Israel, "and I hate a man's covering himself with violence as well as with his garment," says the LORD Almighty.

So guard yourself in your spirit, and do not break faith. Malachi 2:15–16 (NIV)

First seek the counsel of the LORD. 1 Kings 22:5b (NIV)

Do not let any unwholesome talk come out of your mouths, but only what is helpful for building others up according to their needs, that it may benefit those who listen. Ephesians 4:29 (NIV)

For we walk by faith, not by sight. 2 Corinthians 5:7 (NKJV)

PRAYER: *Dear Lord, my daughter and her husband are talking about divorce. Help them to realize why You hate divorce. May she and her husband remember the vows they took on their wedding day—to live together "until death part us." May they never be unfaithful to each other.*

May our children consider the consequences of divorcing one another, consequences to themselves and to their children—consequences which will affect their offspring emotionally and spiritually. Please send to them those who will minister to them and give them godly counsel that is based on Your holy Word.

Dear God, please help me to be the mother and mother-in-law I should be during this time. Help me to keep a watch over my lips and not let any unwholesome communication come from my mouth. Lord, I pledge to pray for them morning, noon, and night during this time. I pray that they will seek Your will and not make decisions based on feelings. May they walk by faith and not by sight. In Jesus' name, amen.

STRUGGLING FINANCIALLY

Do not be anxious about anything, but in everything, by prayer and petition, with thanksgiving, present your requests to God. And the peace of God, which transcends all understanding, will guard your hearts and your minds in Christ Jesus. . . . And my God will meet all your needs according to His glorious riches in Christ Jesus. Philippians 4:6–7, 19 (NIV)

"No one can serve two masters. Either he will hate the one and love the other, or he will be devoted to the one and despise the other. You cannot serve both God and Money. Therefore I tell you, do not worry about your life, what you will eat or drink; or about your body, what you will wear. Is not life more important than food, and the body more important than clothes? Look at the birds of the air; they do not sow or reap or store away in barns, and yet your heavenly Father feeds them. Are you not much more valuable than they? Who of you by worrying can add a single hour to his life? And why do you worry about clothes? See how the lilies of the field grow. They do not labor or spin. Yet I tell you that not even Solomon in all his splendor was dressed like one of these." Matthew 6:24–29 (NIV)

But godliness with contentment is great gain. For we brought nothing into the world, and we can take nothing out of it. But if we have food and clothing, we will be content with that. People who want to get rich fall into temptation and a trap and into many foolish and harmful desires that plunge men into ruin and destruction. For the love of money is a root of all kinds of evil. Some people, eager for money, have wandered from the faith and pierced themselves with many griefs. But you, man of God, flee from all this, and pursue righteousness, godliness, faith, love, endurance and gentleness. Fight the good fight of the faith. Take hold of the eternal life to which you were called when you made your good confession in the presence of many witnesses. 1 Timothy 6:6–12 (NIV)

But you shall remember the Lord your God, for it is He who is giving you power to make wealth. Deuteronomy 8:18

PRAYER: *Oh Father, I don't have to tell You that my children are struggling financially right now. Lord, forgive me for being anxious about it. You have told us to be anxious for nothing, but to bring every detail of our needs to You in earnest and thankful prayer. That is what I am doing now. I ask that You supply their needs today. I am not asking for their wants to be met, just their needs. As You feed the birds of the air, I ask that You provide food and shelter for my children.*

You are the One who gives the power to make wealth. Please help _____ and _____ to be careful with the money You provide for them and help them choose never to live beyond their means. Keep them from the love of money and help them to be content. Teach them to pursue righteousness, godliness, faith, love, endurance, and gentleness. All these things I pray in the name of Jesus, amen.

FORGET-ME-NOT

Constancy

FORGET-ME-NOT
Constancy

"The forget-me-not speaks the heart message of *constancy*." Constancy requires one to be faithful and obedient to the Lord in the times when all are looking on and in the times when no one is looking. "Every day is the time to be constant and faithful to the Master. . . . Those who in trust call upon the name of the Lord Jesus, who have accepted His salvation by grace through faith, are enlisted in His service for life—for every day of life."[6] They will find their joy in endless devotion which results in walking in the light, exemplifying godly character, day in and day out.

CHAPTER 6
PRAYERS FOR MY CHILD'S CHARACTER DEVELOPMENT

For this reason I bow my knees before the Father, . . . that He would grant you, according to the riches of His glory, to be strengthened with power through His Spirit in the inner man. Ephesians 3:14, 16

Godly character is foundational. Thus, we must pray for the development of character qualities in the lives of our children. The ones we have chosen are essential for spiritual development. You may desire to add more God-like traits to this list as you read and study God's Word.

DILIGENCE

The hand of the diligent will rule,
But the slack *hand* will be put to forced labor.
Proverbs 12:24

Whatever your hand finds to do, verily, do it with all your might. Ecclesiastes 9:10

And whatever you do in word or deed, do all in the name of the Lord Jesus. . . . Whatever you do, do your work heartily, as for the Lord rather than for men. Colossians 3:17, 23

Therefore, my beloved brethren, be steadfast, immovable, always abounding in the work of the Lord, knowing that your toil is not in vain in the Lord. 1 Corinthians 15:58

With good will render service, as to the Lord and not to men. Ephesians 6:7

PRAYER: *Dear Heavenly Father, I pray that my child will be diligent in _____ (whatever his task may be). May he do this work with all his might, giving his very best effort. May he see his work as being done for You and for Your glory. May he be more concerned about pleasing You than he is about pleasing others. Please help him not to give up easily, but to persevere. May he be steadfast and immovable, abounding in his work, knowing that his toil will not be in vain if it is done to please You. May he exemplify godly character, day in and day out. In Jesus' name I pray, amen.*

DISCERNMENT

So give your servant a discerning heart to govern your people and to distinguish between right and wrong. 1 Kings 3:9–10 (NIV)

> Teach me knowledge and good judgment,
>   for I believe in your commands.
> Psalm 119:66 (NIV)

But solid food is for the mature, who because of practice have their senses trained to discern good and evil. Hebrews 5:14

PRAYER: *Father God, I ask for discernment for my child. I ask that he will constantly partake of the solid food of Your Word, so that*

he will train his senses to discern between good and evil, right and wrong. In Jesus' sweet name, amen.

DISCIPLINE

Apply your heart to discipline,
　　And your ears to words of knowledge.
　　Proverbs 23:12

Like a city that is broken into and without walls
　　Is a man who has no control over his spirit.
　　Proverbs 25:28

Now for this very reason also, applying all diligence, in your faith supply moral excellence, and in your moral excellence, knowledge, and in your knowledge, self-control, and in your self-control, perseverance, and in your perseverance, godliness. 2 Peter 1:5–6

But solid food is for the mature, who because of practice have their senses trained to discern good and evil. Hebrews 5:14

Discipline yourself for the purpose of godliness. 1 Timothy 4:7b

PRAYER: *Oh our God, how I pray that my child will apply her heart to be disciplined. May she be disciplined physically, exercising self-control and diligence in the way she takes care of her body. May she be disciplined mentally, utilizing her mind to the fullest in the endeavors she undertakes. May she discipline her senses to discern between good and evil, and thereby make wise choices each day of her life. Emotionally, may she learn to control her spirit, so that she will never be like a city that is broken into and without walls. May she discipline herself for the purpose of godliness. In Jesus' name, amen.*

HONESTY

The Lord detests lying lips,
    but He delights in men who are truthful.
    Proverbs 12:22 (NIV)

A fortune made by a lying tongue
    is a fleeting vapor and a deadly snare.
    Proverbs 21:6 (NIV)

A false witness will perish,
    but the man who listens to the truth
    will speak forever.
    Proverbs 21:28

Pray for us, for we are sure that we have a good conscience, desiring to conduct ourselves honorably in all things. Hebrews 13:18

"You know the commandments, 'DO NOT MURDER, DO NOT COMMIT ADULTERY, DO NOT STEAL, DO NOT BEAR FALSE WITNESS.'" Mark 10:19

There are six things which the Lord hates,
Yes, seven which are abomination to Him:
Haughty eyes, a lying tongue, . . .
A false witness *who* utters lies.
   Proverbs 6:16–17a, 19a

And just as you want people to treat you, treat them in the same way. Luke 6:31

PRAYER: *Dear Lord, how I pray that my child will learn early the importance of being honest, of telling the truth, of giving a true account of the happenings in his life. May he have a deep desire to consistently keep a good conscience and choose to conduct himself honorably in all things. May he deal fairly and honestly with others, just as he would like to have them deal with him. May he learn to hate the things You hate, O God. May he also realize that You delight in those who are truthful, and so will bless him as he practices honesty in word and deed. In Jesus' name I pray, amen.*

INTEGRITY

He who walks in integrity walks securely,
But he who perverts his ways will be found out.
   Proverbs 10:9

The integrity of the upright will guide them,
But the falseness of the treacherous will destroy them.
   Proverbs 11:3

A righteous man who walks in his integrity—
How blessed are his sons after him.
    Proverbs 20:7

"Far be it from me that I should declare you right;
Till I die I will not put away my integrity from me."
    Job 27:5

PRAYER: *Oh Lord, I know You want _____ to be a person of integrity. You tell us that the righteous who walk in integrity will have children who are blessed. May she learn early to walk only in the counsel of godly, upright friends, realizing that the integrity of the upright will guide her properly, but the falseness of the treacherous will destroy her. May she have the right mentors who will teach her Your ways.*

May her lips not speak unjustly and may her tongue not utter deceit. May she realize that she who lives with integrity walks securely, but she who perverts her ways will be found out. May she, like Job, determine that for as long as she lives, she will maintain her integrity. May it be said of her as it was of Daniel: "They could find no ground of accusation or evidence of corruption, inasmuch as he was faithful, and no negligence or corruption was to be found in him" (Daniel 6:4). Thank You, Lord. In Jesus' name, amen.

HUMILITY

When pride comes, then comes disgrace,
    but with humility comes wisdom.
    Proverbs 11:2 (NIV)

"This is the one I esteem:
   he who is humble and contrite in spirit,
   and trembles at my word."
   Isaiah 66:2b (NIV)

"For I am gentle and humble in heart." Matthew 11:29b (NIV)

Do nothing out of selfish ambition or vain conceit, but in humility consider others better than yourselves. Philippians 2:3 (NIV)

If you are wise, live a life of steady goodness, so that only good deeds will pour forth. And if you don't brag about them, then you will be truly wise! James 3:13 (TLB)

"God opposes the proud but gives grace to the humble." . . . Humble yourselves before the Lord, and He will lift you up. James 4:6b, 10 (NIV)

PRAYER: *Oh Jesus, just as You were humble in heart, You said that You esteem those who are humble and contrite of heart. You even told us that if we would humble ourselves, You would lift us up. Thank You for giving grace and wisdom to the humble.*

I ask that You show me how to teach my child to be humble like You. Help him to realize that his good deeds come from godly character; therefore he should not brag about them. Teach him to do nothing out of selfish ambition or vain conceit, but in humility to consider others better than himself. In Jesus' name, amen.

MEEKNESS

But the meek will inherit the land
and enjoy great peace.
Psalm 37:11 (NIV)

"Blessed are the meek,
for they will inherit the earth."
Matthew 5:5 (NIV)

PRAYER: *Jesus, I ask that my child not be arrogant, but meek. Father, show him how to demonstrate a meek spirit, just as You did when You lived on earth. In Your name, amen.*

KINDNESS AND GENTLENESS

A gentle answer turns away wrath,
but a harsh word stirs up anger.
Proverbs 15:1 (NIV)

"Take my yoke upon you and learn from me, for I am gentle and humble in heart, and you will find rest for your souls." Matthew 11:29 (NIV)

Love is patient, love is kind. 1 Corinthians 13:4a (NIV)

Be kind and compassionate to one another, forgiving each other, just as in Christ God forgave you. Ephesians 4:32 (NIV)

Let your gentleness be evident to all. The Lord is near. Philippians 4:5 (NIV)

Make sure that nobody pays back wrong for wrong, but always try to be kind to each other and to everyone else. 1 Thessalonians 5:15 (NIV)

And so, as those who have been chosen of God, holy and beloved, put on a heart of compassion, kindness, humility, gentleness and patience. Colossians 3:12

PRAYER: *O Jesus, we know that You were gentle, that You admonished us to clothe ourselves in kindness and gentleness. You teach us that we are to be kind and compassionate, forgiving others.*

We are to let our gentleness be evident to all and to be kind to each other, giving gentle answers. Lord, please show me how to model this before my children so that they learn to be like You, gentle and kind. In the gentle name of Jesus I pray, amen.

SEXUAL PURITY

Flee immorality. Every other sin that a man commits is outside the body, but the immoral man sins against his own body. Or do you not know that your body is a temple of the Holy Spirit who is in you, whom you have from God, and that you are not your own? For you have been bought with a price; therefore glorify God in your body. 1 Corinthians 6:18–20

For this is the will of God, your sanctification; that is, that you abstain from sexual immorality. 1 Thessalonians 4:3

Now flee from youthful lusts, and pursue righteousness, faith, love and peace with those who call on the Lord from a pure heart. 2 Timothy 2:22

Watch over your heart with all diligence,
For from it flow the springs of life.
Proverbs 4:23

Do not enter the path of the wicked,
And do not proceed in the way of evil men.
Proverbs 4:14

For the Lord will be your confidence,
And will keep your foot from being caught.
Proverbs 3:26

PRAYER: *My Lord, please hear me today. Only You, through the power of Your Holy Spirit, can enable my child to be victorious in the area of sexual purity. Only You can empower her to abstain from immorality.*

How I pray that she will realize that her body is not her own—she has been bought with a price—the price You paid on Calvary for her sins—and her body belongs to Jesus. May she realize that her body is the temple of the Holy Spirit and that she must not defile it. Give her the courage to flee from immorality—to flee from youthful lusts.

May she guard her heart with all diligence so that she will remain pure. Help her to choose her friends wisely and not to be led astray by peers who are evil. Lord, she needs Your help moment by moment. May she seek Your face at every turn in the road on her life's journey. O Lord, how I praise You that when she puts her confidence in You, You can keep her foot from being caught. In Jesus' name, amen.

COSMOS

Aspiration

COSMOS
Aspiration

"The cosmos . . . speaks of *aspiration*. . . .
With a gracious nod it seems to rise above
its surroundings—surroundings which may
be either a well-ordered garden or one full
of weeds—into the spiritual world of
higher things. It seems to be saying to
everything and everybody, 'Heads up! Eyes
to the skies!' The gospel of Jesus Christ . . .
awakens new thoughts, impulses, and
desires. . . . It sets one's soul toward a
higher goal and makes him want to forget
those things which are behind and reach
forth 'unto those things which are before'
as he presses 'toward the mark for the
prize of the high calling of God in Christ
Jesus' (Philippians 3:13–14, KJV)."[7]

CHAPTER 7
PRAYERS FOR MY CHILD AS A STUDENT

Be diligent to present yourself approved to God as a workman who does not need to be ashamed, handling accurately the word of truth. 2 Timothy 2:15

From their very first day of school until their last, our children need our intercessory prayers. While we mothers cannot hold our students' hands as they go through their school days, we can always hold them up to their heavenly Father in prayer. Whether they face a test, a false teaching, a temptation, or other types of trials, we need to stand in the gap for our children.

TO APPLY HIMSELF TO HIS WORK

Be diligent to present yourself approved to God as a workman who does not need to be ashamed, handling accurately the word of truth. 2 Timothy 2:15

And whatever you do, whether in word or deed, do it all in the name of the Lord Jesus, giving thanks to God the Father through him. . . . Whatever you do, work at it with all your heart, as working for the Lord, not for men. Colossians 3:17, 23 (NIV)

PRAYER: *I pray that my child will study in a way that will be approved by You. May he be a diligent worker who will never be ashamed in the classroom because of being unprepared. I pray that whatever he does, he will do with all his might, seeking to glorify You, Lord, rather than to please man. In Jesus' name, amen.*

TO HOLD FAST TO HER BELIEF IN GOD

Then he taught me and said to me,
"Let your heart hold fast my words;
Keep my commandments and live."
    Proverbs 4:4

For this reason also, since the day we heard of it, we have not ceased to pray for you and to ask that you may be filled with the knowledge of His will in all spiritual wisdom and understanding, so that you may walk in a manner worthy of the Lord, to please Him in all respects. Colossians 1:9–10a

PRAYER: *God, I pray that my child may hold fast to her belief in You. May she remember what we have taught her about You. May she obey Your commandments. May she seek Your will daily and thus be filled with the knowledge of Your will in all spiritual wisdom and understanding. I ask all these things so that she will walk in a manner worthy of You, pleasing You in all respects. In Jesus' name, amen.*

TO SHOW RESPECT FOR AUTHORITY

For rebellion is as the sin of divination,
And insubordination is as iniquity and idolatry.
    1 Samuel 15:23

PRAYER: *Dearest Lord, I pray that _____ will be respectful of the school authorities. We have tried to teach him respect for those over him, but we know that some of the school rules may not be easy for him to follow. Keep him from becoming rebellious and insubordinate. In Jesus' sweet name, amen.*

TO ACCEPT DISCIPLINE AND PROFIT FROM IT

My son, do not reject the discipline of the LORD
Or loathe His reproof,
For whom the LORD loves He reproves,
Even as a father, the son in whom he delights.
  Proverbs 3:11–12

He who heeds discipline shows the way to life,
  but whoever ignores correction leads others
  astray. Proverbs 10:17 (NIV)

PRAYER: *Dear Father, as the need for discipline arises in _____'s life, please help him not to ignore it or reject it, but receive it as something necessary for his development. May the ones administering the discipline do so in love and not in anger. May he profit from it and learn the lessons he needs to learn. In Jesus' name, amen.*

TO BE WELL-ROUNDED

And as for these four youths, God gave them knowledge and intelligence in every branch of literature and wisdom. Daniel 1:17

PRAYER: *Lord, I desire that* _____ *be a well-rounded student. I pray that she will gain knowledge and intelligence in many branches of literature and wisdom. May she excel in the areas where she is gifted, but may she not avoid those other areas of learning and experience that would be good for her. In Jesus' name, amen.*

TO BE KEPT FROM LAZINESS

One who is slack in his work
　　is brother to one who destroys.
　　Proverbs 18:9 (NIV)

Diligent hands will rule,
　　but laziness ends in slave labor.
　　Proverbs 12:24 (NIV)

Laziness brings on deep sleep,
　　and the shiftless man goes hungry.
　　Proverbs 19:15 (NIV)

PRAYER: *Lord, please help my child not to be lazy. Help him to see that one who is slack in his work is a brother to one who destroys. May he realize the kind of life to which laziness leads a person. Use me to help him learn the lessons about diligence that You desire for him to learn. In Jesus' name I pray, amen.*

FOR PROTECTION FROM HOMESICKNESS

"Do not grieve, for the joy of the LORD is your strength."
Nehemiah 8:10b (NIV)

Weeping may endure for a night, but joy *cometh* in the morning. Psalm 30:5b (KJV)

> You have made known to me the path of life;
> you will fill me with joy in your presence.
> Psalm 16:11a (NIV)

To bestow on them . . . the oil of gladness instead of mourning, and a garment of praise instead of a spirit of despair. Isaiah 61:3 (NIV)

PRAYER: *Oh Lord, my daughter is homesick and needs Your help and strength to make it through this difficult time in her life. Please help her to realize that joy does come in the morning. Help her to know that the joy of the Lord will be her strength in the days ahead. May she come into Your presence so that You can fill her with joy. Then her grief will be replaced with gladness and her despair with a garment of praise. In your precious name I pray, amen.*

FOR PROTECTION FROM THE EVIL ONE

"I do not ask Thee to take them out of the world, but to keep them from the evil one." John 17:15

Finally, be strong in the Lord and in his mighty power. Put on the full armor of God so that you can take your stand against the devil's schemes. Ephesians 6:10 (NIV)

PRAYER: *Father, how I pray that You will protect my child from the evil one today at school. May _____ learn*

how to put on the whole armor of God so that she may be able to stand firm against the schemes of the devil. In Jesus' name, amen.
(See other prayers for protection from evil in Chapter 4.)

FOR PROTECTION FROM DRUGS, ALCOHOL, AND TOBACCO

Wine is a mocker, strong drink a brawler,
And whoever is intoxicated by it is not wise.
   Proverbs 20:1

Do not look on the wine when it is red, . . .
At the last it bites like a serpent
And stings like a viper.
Your eyes will see strange things,
And your mind will utter perverse things.
   Proverbs 23:31–33

No temptation has overtaken you but such as is common to man; and God is faithful, who will not allow you to be tempted beyond what you are able, but with the temptation will provide the way of escape also, so that you may be able to endure it. 1 Corinthians 10:13

PRAYER: *Father, please protect my child from getting involved with drugs, alcohol, and tobacco. Father, please strengthen him within so he will be strong enough to resist the pressure to indulge in these very harmful practices. May he look to You for the power and help he needs and not depend on his own strength to resist these temptations. Thank You, Lord, for hearing my earnest prayers. In Jesus' strong name, amen.*

FOR PROTECTION FROM VICTIMIZATION AND MOLESTATION

AND He said to His disciples, "It is inevitable that stumbling blocks should come, but woe to him through whom they come!" Luke 17:1

> The Lord will guard your going out
>   and your coming in,
> From this time forth and forever.
>   Psalm 121:8

> For he will command his angels concerning you
>   to guard you in all your ways.
>   Psalm 91:11 (NIV)

You are from God, little children, and have overcome them; because greater is He who is in you than he who is in the world. 1 John 4:4

PRAYER: *Dear God, in this very dangerous world, how I need You to send Your angels to keep constant guard over my little girl. Protect her from victimization and molestation. Help her to remember the warnings we have given her. As she goes about her daily life, may she be alert to danger and escape from any harm that is about to befall her. I claim Psalm 91 for her this day. How thankful I am that Your presence and power surrounding our daughter are greater than the power of the evil one. In Jesus' name, amen.*

FOR PROTECTION FROM FALSE TEACHINGS

We are no longer to be children, tossed here and there by waves, and carried about by every wind of doctrine, by the trickery of men, by craftiness in deceitful scheming; but speaking the truth in love, we are to grow up in all aspects into Him, who is the head, even Christ. Ephesians 4:14–15

PRAYER: *Oh God, because there are so many false teachers and false teachings, please protect our child's mind. May he not be tossed here and there, misled by different teachings, but rather, may he be able to discern between the false and the true.*

When he is being taught that which is false, may it come to our attention so that we can point him to Your truth. May we always speak the truth in love as we show him what is right in Your sight.

Please keep him from being tricked by the deceitful scheming of men. Show us how to insulate him with Your word, so that he will grasp Your truths and grow up to be a godly young man. In Jesus' name, amen.

FOR PROTECTION FROM PREMARITAL SEX

Flee immorality. Every other sin that a man commits is outside the body, but the immoral man sins against his own body. Or do you not know that your body is a temple of the Holy Spirit who is in you, whom you have from God, and that you are not your own? For you have been bought with a price: therefore glorify God in your body. 1 Corinthians 6:18–20

No temptation has overtaken you but such as is common to man; and God is faithful, who will not allow you to be tempted beyond what you are able, but with the temptation will provide the way of escape also, so that you may be able to endure it. 1 Corinthians 10:13

PRAYER: *Dear Lord, I pray that _____ will flee immorality. May she not engage in premarital sex, realizing early in her life that true love waits until marriage. Help her to understand that as a Christian, her body is the temple of the Holy Spirit and thus is not her own. It belongs to You. May she realize the price You have paid for her and make a commitment to glorifying You and You alone with her body.*

Please equip her to resist those who would try to compromise her. May she constantly look to You for that way of escape which You have promised to us in our hour of temptation. In Your name I pray, amen.

FOR HELP ON A TEST

Be diligent to present yourself approved to God as a workman who does not need to be ashamed, handling accurately the word of truth. 2 Timothy 2:15

For God hath not given us the spirit of fear; but of power, and of love, and of a sound mind. 2 Timothy 1:7 (KJV)

When I am afraid, I will trust in Thee. Psalm 56:3 (KJV)

Men without any physical defect, handsome, showing aptitude for every kind of learning, well informed, quick to understand. Daniel 1:4 (NIV)

PRAYER: *Dear Lord, my child has a big test tomorrow. Please help him to study diligently for it. May he study the right material so that when he gets to class, he will be well-informed and quick to understand. I pray that he will boldly look to You for help. May he have a sound mind and place his trust in You. In Jesus' holy name, amen.*

FOR PROTECTION ON A TRIP

Then I proclaimed a fast . . . that we might humble ourselves before our God to seek from Him a safe journey for us, our little ones, and all our possessions. Ezra 8:21

> For he will command his angels concerning you
>   to guard you in all your ways.
> Psalm 91:11 (NIV)

PRAYER: *Dear heavenly Father, _____ is traveling to _____ today (or tomorrow). Please give him a safe journey. Keep him from being hurt or harmed in any way. Please command Your angels to guard him everywhere he goes. In Jesus' name I pray, amen.*

FOR HEALTHY RELATIONSHIPS WITH PEERS

Make sure that nobody pays back wrong for wrong, but always try to be kind to each other and to everyone else. 1 Thessalonians 5:15 (NIV)

"But I tell you who hear me: Love your enemies, do good to those who hate you, bless those who curse you, pray for those who mistreat you." Luke 6:27–28 (NIV)

Do not repay anyone evil for evil. Be careful to do what is right in the eyes of everybody. If it is possible, as far as it depends on you, live at peace with everyone. Do not take revenge, my friends, but leave room for God's wrath, for it is written: "It is mine to avenge; I will repay," says the Lord. Romans 12:17–19 (NIV)

PRAYER: *Father, I ask that You help my child to have good, healthy relationships with her peers. Help her to have the courage to follow Your teachings. When she wants to be vengeful because someone has treated her unfairly or unkindly, give her the grace to treat that person with kindness. When she has enemies, show her how to be good to those who hate her and to pray for those who mistreat her. Give her the strength and wisdom to trust You because You tell us that vengeance is Yours.*

Father, when she shares how others have hurt her, I ask You to help me to be an example of Your teaching. Thank You. In Jesus' name, amen.

FOR THE STRENGTH TO STAND ALONE

Finally, be strong in the Lord and in His mighty power. Put on the full armor of God so that you can take your stand against the devil's schemes. . . . Therefore put on the full armor of God so that when the day of evil comes, you may be able to stand your ground, and after you have done everything, to stand. Ephesians 6:10–11, 13 (NIV)

No temptation has seized you except what is common to man. And God is faithful; he will not let you be tempted beyond what you can bear. But when you are tempted, he will also provide a way out so that you can stand up under it. 1 Corinthians 10:13 (NIV)

PRAYER: *Dearest Lord, You have taught us that our strength is found in You and in Your power. How I pray today that as _____ faces temptations to give in to the world's pressures, he will arm himself with your full armor so that he can stand against the devil's schemes. May he stand his ground, believing that You will provide a way of escape, no matter how difficult or unpopular it may be. In Jesus' name, amen.*

FOR TEACHERS AND COACHES

I urge you to live a life worthy of the calling you have received. Ephesians 4:1 (NIV)

Be persistent whether the time is favorable or unfavorable; convince, rebuke, and encourage, with the utmost patience in teaching. 2 Timothy 4:2 (NRSV)

See to it that no one takes you captive through hollow and deceptive philosophy, which depends on human tradition and the basic principles of this world rather than on Christ. Colossians 2:8 (NIV)

Let your speech always be gracious, seasoned with salt, so that you may know how you ought to answer everyone. Colossians 4:6 (NRSV)

And the Lord's servant must not quarrel; instead, he must be kind to everyone, able to teach, not resentful. Those who oppose him he must gently instruct. 2 Timothy 2:24–25b (NIV)

If any of you lacks wisdom, he should ask God, who gives generously to all without finding fault, and it will be given to him. . . . My dear brothers, take note of this: Everyone should be quick to listen, slow to speak and slow to become angry, for man's anger does not bring about the righteous life that God desires. James 1:5, 19–20 (NIV)

PRAYER: *Dear God, show me how to pray for my child's teachers (coaches). I thank You that You have called them to teach. When they are teaching a philosophy that is not godly, please reveal the truth to them so they might teach truth, not ungodliness. Please show them how to live lives worthy of Your calling. I ask You to help them to be kind and not quarrelsome, able to teach, not resentful.*

I pray that their conversation will be gracious, even in opposition and confrontation. Give them the wisdom to gently instruct. When students are upset or angry about a situation, show teachers how to listen.

Show me how to model godly characteristics both to my children and to those who instruct them. In Jesus' name, amen.

FOR LEADERS AND TEACHERS AT CHURCH

For this reason since the day we heard about you, we have not stopped praying for you and asking God to fill you with the knowledge of his will through all spiritual wisdom and understanding. And we pray this in order that you may live a life worthy of the Lord and may please him in every way: bearing fruit in every good work, growing in the knowledge of God, being strengthened with all power according to his glorious might so that you may have great endurance and patience, and joyfully giving thanks to the Father, who has qualified you to share in the inheritance of the saints in the kingdom of light. Colossians 1:9–12 (NIV)

Therefore, as God's chosen people, holy and dearly loved, clothe yourselves with compassion, kindness, humility, gentleness and patience. Bear with each other and forgive whatever grievances you may have against one another. Forgive as the Lord forgave you. And over all these virtues put on love, which binds them all together in perfect unity. . . . And whatever you do, whether in word or deed, do it all in the name of the Lord Jesus, giving thanks to God the Father through him. Colossians 3:12–14, 17 (NIV)

Devote yourselves to prayer, being watchful and thankful. . . . Be wise in the way you act toward outsiders; make the most of every opportunity. Let your conversation be always full of grace, seasoned with salt, so that you may know how to answer everyone. Colossians 4:2, 5–6 (NIV)

PRAYER: *Thank You Father for our child's leaders and teachers at church. I am asking You, Holy Father, to fill them with the knowledge of Your will through all spiritual wisdom and understanding. I pray this in order that they will live their lives worthy of Your Son, Jesus, and will please Him in every way. I ask that they will bear fruit in every good work, and that they will continue to grow in their knowledge of You. I pray for them to be strengthened with power that comes from Jesus, so that they will have endurance and patience. Help them to be men and women of prayer, wise, and able to make the most of every opportunity. I ask that You teach them to have conversations that are always full of grace, seasoned with salt, so that they will know how to answer everyone. In Jesus' name, amen.*

PETUNIA

Happiness

I praise you because I am fearfully
   and wonderfully made;
   your works are wonderful,
   I know that full well.
My frame was not hidden from you
   when I was made in the secret place.
When I was woven together in the
   depths of the earth,
   your eyes saw my unformed body.
All the days ordained for me
   were written in your book
   before one of them came to be.
How precious to me are your thoughts, O God!
How vast is the sum of them!
   Psalm 139:13–17 (NIV)

Train up a child in the way he should go,
Even when he is old he will not depart from it.
   Proverbs 22:6

Pray for us . . . that we will be delivered from wicked and evil men; for not everyone has faith. But the Lord is faithful, and he will strengthen and protect you from the evil one. 2 Thessalonians 3:1–3 (NIV)

For He will give His angels charge concerning you,
To guard you in all your ways.
They will bear you up in their hands,
Lest you strike your foot against a stone.
   Psalm 91:11–12

PRAYER: *Heavenly Father, I come to You with a grateful heart for Your wonderful goodness to me. Thank You for answering my prayers in the gift of this child. She is fearfully and wonderfully made—exactly as You meant her to be. You formed her in my womb and have written in Your book all the days that are ordained for her. I give her to You this day to use in Your service for as long as she lives. Because she is an arrow in my quiver, may I teach and train her in the way she should go so that when she is old, she will not depart from Your teachings.*

I pray that You will stand by her and protect her from the evil one and evil men. Please give Your angels charge concerning my precious child, to guard her in all her ways, bearing her up in their hands so that she will not be harmed. In Jesus' precious name, amen.

FIRST DAY OF SCHOOL

Beloved, I pray that in all respects you may prosper and be in good health, just as your soul prospers. 3 John 2

And Jesus grew in wisdom and stature and in favor with God and men. Luke 2:52 (NIV)

I have no greater joy than to hear that my children are walking in the truth. 3 John 4 (NIV)

And as for these four youths, God gave them knowledge and intelligence in every branch of literature and wisdom. Daniel 1:17

Therefore, my beloved brethren, be steadfast, immovable, always abounding in the work of the Lord, knowing that your labor is not in vain in the Lord. 1 Corinthians 15:58 (NKJV)

PRAYER: *I pray that _____ will be physically, mentally, emotionally, and spiritually a healthy child. May he come to know You as Savior and Lord at an early age so that all his life he may walk in the truth. May he, like Jesus, increase in wisdom and stature and in favor with You and others. May he be a well-rounded person, gaining knowledge and intelligence in every field of literature and wisdom. May he be steadfast and strong, always abounding in Your work, O Lord, all the days of his life. And I will give You all the praise and the glory in Jesus' name, amen.*

GRADUATION DAY

Knowledge makes arrogant, but love edifies. If anyone supposes that he knows anything, he has not yet known as he ought to know; but if anyone loves God, he is known by Him. 1 Corinthians 8:1b–3

Be diligent to present yourself approved to God as a workman who does not need to be ashamed, handling accurately the word of truth. . . . Now flee from youthful lusts, and pursue righteousness, faith, love and peace, with those who call on the Lord from a pure heart. But refuse foolish and ignorant speculations, knowing that they produce quarrels. And the Lord's bond-servant must not be quarrelsome, but be kind to all, able to teach, patient when wronged. 2 Timothy 2:15, 22–24

"But the Helper, the Holy Spirit, whom the Father will send in My name, He will teach you all things and bring to your remembrance all that I said to you." John 14:26

We have not ceased to pray for you and to ask that you may be filled with the knowledge of His will in all spiritual wisdom and understanding. Colossians 1:9b

PRAYER: *Father, as my child graduates, I ask that You help her to remember that knowledge can make her arrogant, but love builds up. May my daughter be diligent to present herself approved to You, God, as a worker who does not need to be ashamed. May she accurately handle Your Word.*

May she flee youthful lusts and pursue righteousness, faith, love, and peace. May she, as one who belongs to You, abstain from wickedness so that she can be a woman of honor who is useful to You.

Help her not to be quarrelsome, but kind to everyone, able to teach, and patient when wronged. Please help her always to look to the Holy Spirit as her Helper, to teach her what she needs to know and to bring to her remembrance the words of Jesus. May she be filled with the knowledge of Your will in all spiritual wisdom and understanding. In Jesus' name, amen.

CELEBRATION OF A NEW JOB OR CAREER

Whatever you do, work at it with all your heart, as working for the Lord, not for men, since you know that you will receive an inheritance from the Lord as a reward. It is the Lord Christ you are serving. Colossians 3:23 (NIV)

Rejoice in the Lord always. I will say it again: Rejoice! . . . And my God will meet all your needs according to his glorious riches in Christ Jesus. Philippians 4:4, 19 (NIV)

PRAYER: *Dear Father, thank You for _____'s new job. We rejoice that You have supplied our child's needs by providing this work. We ask that You help him to do his work each day as if he were*

serving You and not man. Help him to honor You in all he does. In Jesus' name, amen.

WEDDING DAY

"Haven't you read," he replied, "that at the beginning the Creator 'made them male and female,' and said, 'For this reason a man will leave his father and mother and be united to his wife, and the two will become one flesh'? So they are no longer two, but one. Therefore what God has joined together, let man not separate." Matthew 19:4–6 (NIV)

And this is my prayer: that your love may abound more and more in knowledge and depth of insight, so that you may be able to discern what is best and may be pure and blameless until the day of Christ, filled with the fruit of righteousness that comes through Jesus Christ—to the glory and praise of God. Philippians 1:9–11 (NIV)

PRAYER: *Father, the day we have prayed for is here. Thank You for this wedding day. Thank You for bringing _____ into our child's life. Give us wisdom to allow them to establish their home without our interference. Give us wisdom to allow them to leave their parents and be united to each other. Show me when I am a hindrance. I want to obey Your teachings.*

May this young couple truly become one *in heart and mind. May their love abound more and more in knowledge and depth of insight. Help them to discern what is best and to be pure and blameless in Your sight. May they be filled with the fruit of righteousness which comes from knowing You, O Christ. May they be devoted to each other for as long as they both shall live. In Jesus' name, amen.*

(See also the other prayers for marriage on pages 12–15.)

SUNFLOWER

Reverence

SUNFLOWER

Reverence

The sunflower "constantly gazes upon the object of its affection, the sun, and follows it from the moment it rises in the east until it sets in the west, drawing daily sustenance and abounding joy from such reverent worship. The sunflower, by its daily life, seems to be saying to every trusting heart, 'You, too, have a [Son] to gaze upon in wonder and admiration—"the [Son] of Righteousness." Look up! Behold him in all his majesty and beauty!'"[9] "For Christ has entered into heaven itself to appear now before God as our Advocate" (Hebrews 9:24, NLT).

CHAPTER 9
PRAYING WHEN I DON'T KNOW HOW TO PRAY

In the same way, the Spirit helps us in our weakness. We do not know what we ought to pray, but the Spirit himself intercedes for us with groans that words cannot express. And he who searches our hearts knows the mind of the Spirit, because the Spirit intercedes for the saints in accordance with God's will. Romans 8:26–27 (NIV)

As the sunflower depends on the sun, so can we depend on the Son of Righteousness, Jesus Christ, to intercede for us when we do not know how to pray. God's Word tells us that Jesus always lives to intercede for us. (See Hebrews 7:25b.)

> Why are you downcast, O my soul?
> Why so disturbed within me?
> Put your hope in God,
>   for I will yet praise him,
>   my Savior and my God.
> Psalm 43:5 (NIV)

"For I know the plans I have for you," declares the Lord, "plans to prosper you and not to harm you, plans to give you hope and a future. Then you will call upon me and come and pray to me and I will listen to you. You will seek me and find me when you seek me with all your heart." Jeremiah 29:11–13 (NIV)

And in the same way the Spirit also helps our weakness; for we do not know how to pray as we should, but the Spirit Himself intercedes for us with groanings too deep for words; and He who searches the hearts knows what the mind of the Spirit is, because He intercedes for the saints according to the will of God. Romans 8:26–27

PRAYER: *Holy Spirit, thank You for helping me in my weakness. I do not know how to pray in this situation. I call on You so that You will search my heart. Thank You that You are interceding for me in this matter according to God's will. Thank You, God, that You have plans for my child that will give him a future and a hope. Thank You that when I seek You I find You. In Jesus' holy name, amen.*

CHRYSANTHEMUM

Thankfulness

CHRYSANTHEMUM

Thankfulness

"The fall season . . . is really a time of fruition and glory. It produces a radiant flower which spreads abroad the message of cheerfulness—the chrysanthemum. . . . It seems to be urging one to look for the sunlight which God sends into every day. It reminds those who look upon it that God is glorified, not by groans but by thanksgivings, as it puts the heart in tune to sing His praises. It seems to urge one to 'rejoice in the Lord alway' (Philippians 4:4)."[10]

CHAPTER 10
IT'S ALWAYS TIME TO PRAISE THE LORD!

Let everything that has breath praise the Lord.
Praise the Lord. Psalm 150:6 (NIV)

God tells us to praise Him. Psalm 147:1 states that it is good to sing praises to our God. As I praise the Lord and thank Him in all circumstances, I find that I focus my attention on who He is and His power; on His characteristics and not my circumstances. It is good to praise the Lord; as I praise Him, He is glorified.

As you express your praise and gratitude to the Lord, there are many verses in the Bible that you can pray back to Him. We have listed some examples below with a sample prayer. As you look for praise verses, especially in the Psalms, you will discover many others that can be used to honor the Lord in praise and thanksgiving.

> You are worthy, our Lord and God,
> to receive glory and honor and power,
> for you created all things,
> and by your will they were created
> and have their being.
> Revelation 4:11 (NIV)

Do not be anxious about anything, but in everything, by prayer and petition, with thanksgiving, present your requests to God. And the peace of God, which transcends all understanding, will guard your hearts and your minds in Christ Jesus. Philippians 4:6–7 (NIV)

Give thanks in all circumstances, for this is God's will for you in Christ Jesus. 1 Thessalonians 5:18 (NIV)

> Though the fig tree does not bud
>> and there are no grapes on the vines,
> though the olive crop fails
>> and the fields produce no food,
> though there are no sheep in the pen
>> and no cattle in the stalls,
> yet I will rejoice in the LORD,
>> I will be joyful in God my Savior.
> The Sovereign LORD is my strength;
>> he makes my feet like the feet of a deer,
>> he enables me to go on the heights.
>> Habakkuk 3:17–19 (NIV)

> "I am the Lord; that is my name!
>> I will not give my glory to another
>> or my praise to idols."
>> Isaiah 42:8 (NIV)

> The Lord is my strength and my song;
>> he has become my salvation.
> He is my God, and I will praise him,
>> my father's God, and I will exalt him.
>> Exodus 15:2 (NIV)

O my Strength, I sing praise to you;
   you, O God, are my fortress, my loving God.
   Psalm 59:17 (NIV)

I will praise you, O Lord my God, with all my
   heart;
I will glorify your name forever.
   Psalm 86:12 (NIV)

Praise the Lord, O my soul;
   all my inmost being, praise his holy name.
Praise the Lord, O my soul,
   and forget not all his benefits,
who forgives all your sins
   and heals all your diseases,
who redeems your life from the pit
   and crowns you with love and compassion,
who satisfies your desires with good things
   so that your youth is renewed like the eagle's.
   Psalm 103:1–5 (NIV)

Great is the Lord and most worthy of praise;
   his greatness no one can fathom.
   Psalm 145:3 (NIV)

Glorify the Lord with me;
   let us exalt his name together.
   Psalm 34:3 (NIV)

Praise be to the God and Father of our Lord Jesus Christ, who has blessed us in the heavenly realms with every spiritual blessing in Christ. Ephesians 1:3 (NIV)

When he came near the place where the road goes down the Mount of Olives, the whole crowd of disciples began joyfully to praise God in loud voices for all the miracles they had seen: "Blessed is the king who comes in the name of the Lord!" "Peace in heaven and glory in the highest!" Some of the Pharisees in the crowd said to Jesus, "Teacher, rebuke your disciples!" "I tell you," he replied, "if they keep quiet, the stones will cry out." Luke 19:37–40 (NIV)

PRAYER: *God, I praise You. You alone are worthy to receive glory, honor, and power for You created all things. Help me to be obedient, to praise Your name, and to give You all honor and glory. I desire to be thankful in all circumstances, even those that are difficult. When I do not understand all that is happening, my desire is to be obedient and praise You thankfully. You alone are my strength and song. I exalt You. You are so worthy of praise that if I do not praise You, the rocks will cry out. Hallelujah! In Jesus' holy name, amen.*

ENDNOTES

1. Outlaw, Nell Warren, *Voiceless Lips* (Nashville: Broadman Press, 1949), 119–121.

2. Ibid, 30–31.

3. Ibid, 93–96.

4. Ibid, 11, 14.

5. Ibid, 52–53.

6. Ibid, 75, 77.

7. Ibid, 61–62.

8. Ibid, 104–106.

9. Ibid, 130–131.

10. Ibid, 69, 71.

JOURNAL